APALACHICOLA BAY

Kevin M. McCarthy

Illustrations by William Trotter

Pineapple Press, Inc.
Sarasota, Florida

Inquiries should be addressed to:

Pineapple Press, Inc.
P.O. Box 3889
Sarasota, Florida 34230
www.pineapplepress.com

Library of Congress Cataloging-in-Publication Data

McCarthy, Kevin.
  Apalachicola Bay / by Kevin M. McCarthy ; illustrations by William Trotter.— 1st ed.
    p. cm.
  Includes bibliographical references and index.
  ISBN 1-56164-299-1 (pbk. : alk. paper)
  1. Apalachicola Bay Region (Fla.)—History, Local. 2. Franklin County (Fla.)—History, Local. 3. Apalachicola Bay Region (Fla.)—Geography. 4. Franklin County (Fla.)—Geography. 5. Historic sites—Florida—Apalachicola Bay Region. 6. Historic sites—Florida—Franklin County. I. Title.

F317.F7.M25 2004
975.9'91—dc22

                                                                    2003027864

First Edition
10 9 8 7 6 5 4 3 2 1

Design by Shé Heaton
Printed in Korea

Contents ◎

7/04

INTRODUCTION

THROUGHOUT THE UNITED STATES, a long-running debate has been taking place between environmentalists and developers, between those who want to restore or preserve the past and those who want to bulldoze historic buildings to make more parking lots and high-rise condominiums. Florida is one of the battlegrounds where short-sighted schemers have been very successful at despoiling the land, draining its swamps, filling in lakes, even straightening out some of its rivers. Only in the last half of the twentieth century did environmentalists like Marjory Stoneman Douglas, Peter Matthiessen, Jeff Ripple, and Jack Rudloe say "enough is enough! Stop destroying our state!"

Several towns around Apalachicola Bay have also fought this never-ending struggle to preserve the area's natural beauty while allowing its citizens to harvest its bounty, whether from the bay or the forest or the islands. For the most part, they have succeeded, although the threat for individuals to make a fast buck at the expense of the long-term health of the area will always be there.

This is the story of places around Apalachicola Bay: their history, their role in the present, and the plans for their future. This area has not only some of the oldest and most important sites in territorial Florida, but also an oyster industry that leads the state and, despite being threatened, has provided a good income to fishermen for many years.

The bay is greatly dependent on its geography: near some of the world's finest beaches, on a waterway teaming with fish and oysters, in a state that ranks number four in terms of U.S. population. Apalachicola Bay is part of a large marine area called the Apalachicola Bay Aquatic Preserve, which was named by Florida officials in 1969 and covers around eighty thousand acres of sovereign submerged lands. This is a technical term referring to lands including, but not limited to, tidal lands, islands, sandbars, shallow banks, and lands farther towards the water than the ordinary or mean high water line, as well as lands beneath navigable freshwater or beneath tidally-influenced waters, which the State of Florida acquired in 1845 by virtue of statehood.

Apalachicola is part of a large drainage area that includes three rivers to the north (the Apalachicola, Chattahoochee, and Flint) and the Gulf of Mexico to the south. These three rivers drain much of Alabama, Georgia, and Florida waters into the Gulf of Mexico. Apalachicola Bay and its river system cover over twenty-one thousand square miles across three states: Florida, Alabama, and Georgia. In Florida, it covers about 2,400 square miles in six counties: Calhoun, Franklin, Gadsden, Gulf, Jackson, and Liberty. This book deals exclusively with Franklin County.

The Apalachicola Bay area is primarily in Franklin County, one of the largest counties in the state, consisting of 545 square miles (or 348,800 acres) that are mainly filled with forests and marshland. The county has about nine thousand residents, who live primarily in two municipalities: Apalachicola and Carrabelle. The population is predicted to grow modestly to around fourteen thousand by 2020 and to over sixteen thousand by 2030.

Because of changing sea levels, the make-up of the bay has changed considerably. Scientists estimate that two hundred thousand years ago sea level was over four hundred feet lower than it is today, and that Florida's coastline was therefore considerably farther into the Gulf of Mexico. The barrier islands of the bay were formed around five thousand years ago, when the sea level was similar to what it is today.

The bay's waters cover around 155,000 acres, consisting of six areas, from west to east: St. Vincent Sound, Apalachicola Bay, the river delta, East Bay, St. George Sound, and Alligator Harbor. Four natural openings from the bay to the Gulf of Mexico allow boats to enter and exit: West Pass, East Pass, Indian Pass, and Dog Island Reef between Alligator Point and Dog Island. A fifth, manmade pass, Sikes Cut, separates St. George Island from Little St. George Island.

The Intracoastal Waterway passes through the area in a twelve-foot-deep channel through St. George Sound, Apalachicola Bay, up the Apalachicola River to Lake Wimico, and then west to St. Andrews Bay. Two bridges move automobile and truck traffic: Apalachicola to

Eastpoint, Eastpoint to St. George Island.

This book describes the four barrier islands, the forest, river, and estuary; some industries important to the area's economy (shrimping, fishing, oystering, cotton, logging, steamboats, and railroads; and six outlying sites (Fort Gadsden, Lanark, St. James Island, Carrabelle, Carrabelle Beach, and Eastpoint). The second half of the book describes the town of Apalachicola: its main hotels, churches, schools, parks, and museums; and some of its main citizens, past and present.

Sometimes when authors research extensively and write about places, they come to dislike those places, having discovered in their nooks and crannies unpleasantries, hidden scandals, unlikable people. That was not the case here as I spent the last several years learning as much about Apalachicola Bay as possible. I found myself on numerous occasions saying such things as "what a beautiful place!" or "those buildings (or people or beaches or swamps) are amazing," whether in Apalachicola's Lafayette Park or Carrabelle's waterfront or Fort Gadsden's perch on the nearby river.

I've also enjoyed centering this book on water: the freshwater of the Apalachicola River, the mixed water of the bay, and the salty water of the Gulf. If—as I more and more believe—water will be the most important issue for Floridians in the twenty-first century, Franklin County can learn much from the rest of the peninsula: what Floridians have done right (protecting thousands of acres above and below water from development and putting them aside for future generations) and what they have done wrong (the destruction of historic sites for the building of high-rises, even parking lots).

To those first-time or even repeat visitors to this "Forgotten Coast" of Florida, you are in for a pleasant surprise. To the residents of Franklin County: good luck maintaining a good balance between development and preservation, especially with regard to the endangered Apalachicola River.

Among the people to thank for helping me in the research for this book are John Hitron, Barbara Holmes, Jimmy Mosconis, Jimmie Nichols, Ken Reynolds, and Marjorie Solomon.

This book is dedicated to the thousands of local residents and frequent visitors who have succeeded in preserving an area far better than most places in this country.

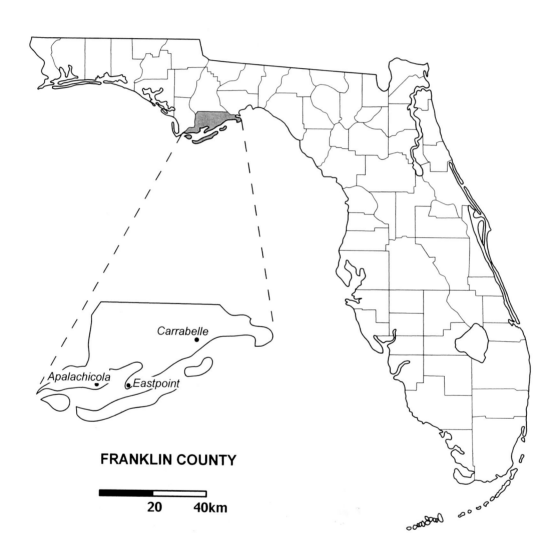

Carrabelle

Apalachicola Eastpoint

FRANKLIN COUNTY

20   40km

I.

APALACHICOLA BAY

A FTER OTHER SECTIONS OF FLORIDA CAME UP WITH catchy descriptions such as "The First Coast," "The Space Coast," and "The Treasure Coast," someone came up with "The Forgotten Coast" to describe the Apalachicola Bay section of the Panhandle. The term "forgotten" refers more to an aspect that was neglected, rather than found and then lost, in vacationers' mad rush for the glitz of South Florida or the miles of pristine beaches toward Pensacola.

The bay has the best of several worlds: four barrier islands, a rich estuary, several picturesque towns, world-class beaches, racial harmony, and a history that has produced two important scientists and a town that prides itself on having restored its elegant houses. That's the good news; the bad news is the potential for serious harm to the bay from forces far away, for example, in Georgia and Alabama, and the threat that large landowners can build new communities that might not preserve the county's natural beauty.

Franklin County, the home of Apalachicola Bay, is one of Florida's smallest in terms of population, with only 9,829 inhabitants. This figure represents a decrease from the 11,057 reported in the 2000 census, which had caused it to rank 64 out of 68 Florida counties. Although the county gained 2,090 residents in the 1980s, all of the increase came from migration into the area; the deaths of the residents actually exceeded the births by 94 (1,211 deaths to 1,117 births). In fact, the county gained only 3,992 residents over the past 30 years or about 111 people a month, whereas demographers note that the state as a whole gained about 900 people a day in that same span of time. Franklin County's population per square mile (21) is one of the lowest in the state, which has 296 per square mile. The county has one of the lowest percentages of residents aged seventeen and under (17.99 percent) compared with the state as a whole (22.81 percent). Most of the people—7,420 residents or 67 percent of the population—live outside the two incorporated towns of Apalachicola and Carrabelle.

The Florida Legislative Council formed Franklin County out of Washington County on February 8, 1832 and named it after statesman-inventor Benjamin Franklin. The land area of the county (over 348,800 acres or about 545 square miles) is less than one percent of the state as a whole, and one-fourth of Franklin County (the Apalachicola National Forest and St. Vincent National Wildlife Refuge) is federally owned. The county's widest point, from near Sumatra to Cape St. George, stretches about twenty-eight miles; its longest point, from Indian Pass to Bald Point in the east, is about fifty-four miles.

The area has a moderate climate thanks to the nearby Gulf of Mexico. In summer (June to September), the average temperature is 80° Fahrenheit because of the breezes from the Gulf and the prevalence of cumulus clouds, which often shade the land without obscuring the sun. In winter, the temperature rises to a manageable 56° Fahrenheit.

Come with us, then, on a tour of the Forgotten Coast, a place that struggles to maintain a working environment with preservation of its past, to grow slowly and keep its natural beauty.

1.

ST. VINCENT ISLAND

"I'm gonna stay/Along the Ap-a-la-chi-co-la-Bay"

—Bing Crosby, "Apalachicola, Florida" (a song)

IMAGINE A BARRIER ISLAND OFF THE COAST OF FLORIDA that has no human residents, only lots of sea turtles, waterfowl, rare Asian Sambar deer, even some red wolves. The island is quite large (twelve thousand square acres), lies just off the coast where very expensive homes face the Gulf of Mexico, and has the potential of becoming full of roads and high-rises and fast-food restaurants. The possibility is alarming. But then you learn that the owner of the island is the U.S. Department of the Interior. You exhale, realizing that it will remain in its pristine form forever. You have there, in a nutshell, a description of St. Vincent Island.

The United States has over five hundred natural refuges, managed by the U.S. Fish and Wildlife Service and encompassing more than ninety million acres of wildlife habitat. St. Vincent National Wildlife Refuge at the western edge of Apalachicola Bay is one of those sites, having been purchased by the Nature Conservancy in 1968, then sold to the Fish and Wildlife Service

Since 1990, scientists have used the isolated St. Vincent's Island to breed endangered red wolves.

of the U.S. Department of the Interior, which manages it as a protected national wildlife refuge.

Water is all around: the Gulf of Mexico to the south and west, St. Vincent Sound to the north, and Apalachicola Bay to the east. The island even has freshwater lakes, which is rare on small Florida islands. Indian Pass, off the northwestern tip, separates the island from the mainland, which is just several hundred yards away but is reachable only by boat. The water there, called St. Vincent Sound, is very shallow (averaging about four feet in depth) and has many oyster beds. Several hundred yards also separate the island from Little St. George Island at the southeast at West Pass. The mainland shore just to the north of Saint Vincent Island is owned by St. Joe Company and is mostly undeveloped, although the company may develop it in the next few decades.

The sea level there and elsewhere in Florida has fluctuated dramatically over the past five thousand years. Thousands of years ago, when large glaciers covered the earth and contained much of the world's water supply, the level of the oceans was as low as 350 feet lower than today. The coastline of Florida, including the Apalachicola Bay area, extended far out into the Gulf of Mexico. About nine thousand years ago, as the climate of the earth warmed up and the glaciers started to melt, the coastline of Florida began to recede to where it is today.

If you were to look at St. Vincent Island from a plane, you'd see a triangle-shaped structure four miles wide at the eastern end and nine miles long, with eighty miles of sand roads running east to west and fourteen miles of beaches along the eastern and southern shores. The topography ranges from freshwater lakes and swamps on the eastern end to dry pine forests on the western end. The climate is mild, with the annual rainfall averaging about fifty-seven inches. Scientists have identified several distinct habitat types on the island: wetlands, which consist of freshwater lakes, streams, and tidal marsh; dunes with live oak and other trees; cabbage palm stands; and four different slash-pine communities.

This barrier island is old, dating back over thirty-five hundred years, although geologists estimate the age of parts of the island to be forty-four hundred years, which would make it one of the oldest barrier islands in Florida. Native Americans lived there two thousand years ago, as indicated by pottery shards. In the early seventeenth century, Franciscan friars working with Apalachee tribes named the island after St. Vincent, a Spanish martyr of the fourth century. After those Native Americans died off from European diseases and battles over the next hundred years, Creeks and Seminoles entered Florida and lived on the island. In 1811, the Native Americans sold the island to the trading house of Panton, Leslie and Company, later known as John Forbes and Company, which sold it to the Carnochan and Mitchel Mercantile House in 1828.

In 1858, the Apalachicola Land Company, which had acquired the island, sold it to local lawyer Robert Floyd. In 1868, George Hatch, a banker, former mayor of Cincinnati, Ohio, and husband of local resident Elizabeth Wefing, bought the island at a public auction for $3,000 and lived there with his family for a time. His grave, located near West Pass Channel and marked with a small, white-cypress fence and stones, is the only marked grave on the island.

From 1878 until 1888, ships that drew no more than eleven feet of water used West Pass, which, at a natural depth of forty to fifty feet, is the deepest pass into the bay today. Shipping out lumber was a profitable business at that time, but the need to use larger ships necessitated the dredging of East Pass to the west of Dog Island.

In 1908, Ray Pierce, a wealthy doctor from Buffalo, New York who had made a fortune from the manufacture of patent medicines and the Pierce Arrow car, bought the island. He built cottages and thirty miles of roads, spent $60,000 importing game animals from Europe, and stayed there with his family and friends in the winter months. During the 1920s, ranchers raised beef cattle on the island and sold them to markets in nearby Apalachicola. In the 1940s, oyster growers leased some of the land.

In 1948, the Loomis brothers of New York City and Virginia bought the island for $140,000 and imported exotic animals such as black bucks, elands (the largest living antelope), ring-

necked pheasants, and zebras. Another exotic animal introduced there was the Sambar deer, an elk from Southeast Asia
similar to the American elk. Visitors can still see the seventy or
so descendants of those deer, which weigh as much as five to six
hundred pounds, easily outweighing the native white-tailed deer,
which average about one hundred pounds. The two species have
managed to co-exist on the island, with the white-tailed deer
preferring the drier, upland habitats, and the Sambar deer stay-
ing in the marshes and other wetlands.

In 1968, the Nature Conservancy bought the island for $2.2
million. Later that year, the U.S. Fish and Wildlife Service
bought it with money raised from its duck stamps. Officials
allow limited, primitive hunting each year in order to control
the populations of certain animals such as the wild pigs and
Sambar deer, but hunters need permits.

When the U.S. government established the refuge in 1968 to
provide habitat for the conservation and protection of all
species of wildlife, it was most concerned about protecting
waterfowl. Since then, however, it has expanded its goal to
include the protection of other species. Among the animals that
find refuge on the island are indigo snakes (which are found in
burrows made by gopher tortoises in the dunes), bald eagles
(which nest in pine trees near the marshes and freshwater lakes),
brown pelicans, and loggerhead sea turtles (which nest on the
undisturbed beaches). Peregrine falcons and wood storks are
among the migrating birds that stop on the island. Over 150 different species of birds have been seen on St. Vincent and St.
George Islands.

As is true elsewhere, the manager of the National Wildlife
Refuge shares its revenue with the local county, in compliance
with a 1978 law that mandates revenue sharing for all lands
administered solely or primarily by the U.S. Fish and Wildlife
Service. The fact that Franklin County earns revenue from the
island (as well as from the Apalachicola National Forest, as is
discussed in chapter five), is important since the island and forest take up a lot of land that could bring in a lot of money if they
were allowed to pass into private hands.

Beginning in 1990, scientists have used the isolated St.

Vincent Island to breed endangered red wolves, animals that were almost hunted to extinction by European settlers and by farmers who feared the animals would harm people or livestock. St. Vincent is only one of four national wildlife areas in the United States where the wolves are brought to live and breed. The island is suitable for such breeding because of its isolation and because the wolves prefer marshes and swamps.

At any one time only two to six wolves are on the island. When they have pups, rangers take the pups to other sites to breed with other red wolves, for example, at North Carolina's Alligator River National Wildlife Refuge or the Great Smoky Mountains National Park on the border of North Carolina and Tennessee. The wolves there are useful in controlling the size of deer populations, which can easily get out of control. On St. Vincent, rangers keep the wolves in a fifty-foot-by-fifty-foot enclosure away from public areas. Such efforts have slowly begun to re-introduce the wolves into the Southeast, where they used to roam freely.

The seasons of the year see different animal populations on the island. The winter (December to February) has the greatest number of waterfowl. At that time, white-tailed bucks are in rut, alligators bask in the sun, and bald eagles and great horned owls start to nest. In the spring (March to May), white-tailed bucks drop their antlers, soft-shelled turtles lay eggs in the sand, wood ducks fly in, ospreys nest around freshwater lakes, and young eagles begin flying. In the summer (June to August), white-tailed bucks roam freely, female alligators guard their young in the marshes, loggerhead sea turtles lay their eggs on the beaches, and swallow-tailed kites and wood storks fly over. In the fall (September to November), white-tailed bucks grow antlers as they prepare to rut, waterfowl and shore birds migrate, and peregrine falcons fly over. The fact that one of the major islands of Apalachicola Bay is now a preserve that should remain undeveloped forever can be largely credited to the foresight of environmental groups in Franklin County.

Today, you can only reach St. Vincent Island by boat, normally from the ramp at the end of SR 30 at Indian Pass, which has a maximum depth of twelve feet and only about three to four hundred yards between the island and the mainland, although the strong rip tides running there prevent most people from swimming across. Many boats and water-bikers make the short trip over to the western end of the island, where the trails begin. Visitors, who may use the island only in the daytime, can fish, hike, bird-watch, photograph, and collect shells. Bicycles are permitted only on the roads. No pets, firearms, weapons, or fireworks are allowed on the island. Visitors may not remove artifacts, plants, or animals.

2.

LITTLE ST. GEORGE ISLAND

"Every brick in the powerful rocketing tower [of the Cape

St. George Lighthouse] was firmly set down and mortared

with a tenacious British stubbornness to defy the sea and the

centuries, and it is the oldest standing work of man in all the

region that it serves and dominates."

—Alexander Key, *Island Light*, 1950

APALACHICOLA BAY HAS TWO LIGHTHOUSES: Crooked River Lighthouse at Carrabelle Beach and Cape St. George Lighthouse on Little St. George Island. The former is high on a hill and fairly safe from Mother Nature; the latter is low on the beach and subject to hurricanes and tidal surges.

The small, nine-mile-long barrier island, located between St. Vincent Island to the west and St. George Island to the east, has two names: Little St. George Island and Cape St. George Island. It could very well be called the Little Island That Could. It has survived the forces of Mother Nature and the meddling of engineers determined to cut it off from its larger parent to the east; it has protected lighthouse keepers' families from the harsh environment; and it shelters the valuable waters of Apalachicola Bay. But it has not had a scar-free history, thanks to humans from the mainland and Mother Nature from the Gulf.

Apalachicola Bay, which the island helps protect, is less than ten thousand years old and has been relatively stable

The Cape St. George Lighthouse has withstood some severe hurricanes.

over the last five thousand years. The two big changes have been the slow but steady southern movement of the Apalachicola River delta and the rise of the sea level, which may have been ten feet or more below the current level forty-five hundred years ago. The barrier islands at the edge of the bay have also been shifting, possibly as much as ten feet a year.

Little St. George Island is part of the Apalachicola National Estuarine Research Reserve and is accessible only by boat. The island is managed as a preserve and it consists of more than eighteen hundred acres. Native Americans occupied the island for hundreds of years before the Europeans arrived in the sixteenth century, as is evidenced by the pottery fragments occasionally found there.

West Gap or New Inlet separates Little St. George from the much larger St. George Island to the east, although silt has occasionally joined the two islands, which have then been separated once again by hurricanes. In the 1950s, the U.S. Army Corps of Engineers made the separation of the two islands more permanent by opening up a pass between them in order to lessen the distance from the town of Apalachicola to the open Gulf for the fishermen who work in the Gulf. The name of the pass, Bob Sikes Cut, honors Florida Congressman Robert "He Coon" Sikes, who represented the area in the U.S. House of Representatives for thirty-eight years. (Also, his wife, Emma, taught school in Apalachicola at one time.) The federal government, which owns the pass, maintains it at a depth of ten feet. Sikes Cut has helped local fishermen greatly, but it has also increased the salinity of the bay, affecting the thriving local oyster business. For the moment, at least, the fishermen have won the battle to keep the pass open.

Little St. George and the other islands in Apalachicola Bay have blunted the force of the hurricanes and protected the mainland, but in doing so, they have often changed shape. For example, a separate island, called Sand Island, occasionally appears after a storm at the western edge of Little St. George. When this happens, more storms and silting cause the few acres that make up Sand Island to be joined once again to Little St. George.

Sand Island has a single tombstone which marks the gravesite of Lewis Leland, a sailor on one of the many ships that used to anchor off the island in the 1840s waiting for barges to bring out lumber from the sawmills on the mainland. When Leland died in 1841 from a disease (probably cholera or yellow fever), his ship was quarantined and he was buried on Sand Island because the townspeople did not want his body in any of their graveyards. Also buried on the island is a horse named Nedd, an animal that helped the lighthouse keepers transport supplies across the island to the keepers' house for many years.

Ten years after the United States acquired La Florida from Spain in 1821, the U.S. Congress authorized the building of a lighthouse on Little St. George, but it took several years for officials to determine who owned what land on the various islands in the bay. Finally, in 1833, workers built the island's first lighthouse at the west end, near the main entrance to the bay.

Mariners, however, realized too late that the lighthouse built on Little St. George was in the wrong place, that the larger Cape St. George often blocked its view, and that the light was too weak to be of much use. Eventually, reason prevailed, and workers built a new, sixty-five-foot-high lighthouse two miles away in 1847–1848. A hurricane toppled that tower in 1851, but a new, seventy-five-foot-tall lighthouse replaced that one the following year. Moving the structure four hundred feet from the shore and building a stronger foundation in 1852 enabled the tower to last till now, but Hurricane Opal nearly toppled it in 1995. Engineers eventually righted it, but erosion continues to threaten it.

Today, the Cape St. George Lighthouse Society has plans to replace the damaged spiral staircase and all the windows and doors in the tower. The society also has hopes of installing a workable light in the tower, not as an aid to navigation, but as a landmark.

As international trade made Apalachicola more important and ships began using the deeper waters at East Pass in the first part of the nineteenth century, local officials lobbied for a new lighthouse to be built on Dog Island. (To learn of their successful efforts, see chapter four.)

Alexander Key's novel, *Island Light,* describes life in and around the lighthouse in the second half of the nineteenth century and the difficult times when the keepers' families did not get along with each other. Key lived in the beautiful yellow house, called the Key House, that can still be seen at 15 13th Street in Apalachicola across from Lafayette Park.

Little St. George and the other islands in the bay saw action during the American Civil War as blockading ships from the Union Navy entered the bay looking for blockade-runners and contraband. In one instance in 1861, Union forces attacked a Confederate ship, the *Finland,* and set it afire when they could not sail it away.

Right after the Civil War, federal troops took over some of the wharves and buildings of Apalachicola as well as some of the offshore islands, including Little St. George, but the federals soon left and the area resumed its commerce and trading. Legend has it that one soldier left the town with no regrets: "Farewell, sandy, dry, hot Apalachicola. May we never see thee more!"

In the five decades after the war, the ownership of Little St. George and the larger St. George Island was never quite clear, other than the federal ownership of the lighthouse property on the former, especially as hurricanes and shifting sands sometimes joined the two islands into one. Thomas Orman, owner of a large part of Little St. George, bought more than fifteen hundred acres of the island in 1861 for about $405, which was less than thirty cents an acre.

In the 1890s, one of the lighthouse keepers on the island, Edward Porter, bought most of the island from the Ormans, built a house and a school, and hired a teacher for his six children and the five children of the assistant keeper. Porter kept two hundred hogs and two hundred cattle, which he raised for the meat that he could sell on the mainland. Whenever a hurricane approached the island, the families would move into what they called a "storm house," a sturdy structure that could withstand the storms that buffeted the bay. Porter also built a small cottage on the eastern end of the island and rented it out to vacationers. The fact that the cottage was very popular with visitors may have instilled the idea that outsiders would find the island very attractive and would be willing to rent vacation homes.

Sixteen years after Porter's death in 1913, his descendants sold the island for $17,500. It might have brought in more money, but the Depression greatly deflated the real estate market in Florida. The island was still useful, even for those who did not want to live there. From time to time, for example, in the periods from 1910 to 1916 and from 1950 to 1956, workers extracted turpentine from the island's pine trees, whose scars can still be seen by visitors.

During World War II, the Gulf waters south of Little St. George hid German U-boats searching for prey. Because those U-boats needed sixty feet of water to operate under the surface, most tanker captains sailed more inland, close to shore. But not all of them. In June, 1942, the captain of the British Liberty Ship *HMS Empire Mica,* which was transporting aviation gas to Great Britain, saw that his ship was drawing too much water and therefore decided to race across deep water late at night to reach a safe port. A U-boat torpedoed the *Mica,* and the large explosion could be seen from the mainland. Boats from Apalachicola sped out to the *Mica,* but could rescue only fourteen of the ship's thirty-three-man crew. Today, the sunken *Mica,* which many consider a living memorial to those who died in the war, has become a reef where thousands of fish attract fishermen and divers.

Visitors to Captain Anderson's Restaurant at 5551 N. Lagoon Drive in Panama City, Florida, can see the *Mica's* 32,000-pound bronze propeller, which divers salvaged from the wreck in 1981. Occasionally, survivors of that wreck return to Apalachicola to thank their rescuers. A British film crew in 1987 cast a wreath on the waters where the wreck took place to honor the dead.

At the western edge of Little St. George is West Pass, on the other side of which is St. Vincent's Island. West Pass, at a natural depth of forty to fifty feet, was frequently used during the nineteenth century, when Apalachicola was an important cotton port. Vessels drawing as much as twelve feet would use this pass, but even they had to anchor several miles from shore and wait for smaller boats to unload them and furnish them with outgoing cargo. In 1848, the port shipped more than eighty-five thousand bales to markets. The silt from the Apalachicola River, however, kept filling in parts of the bay, and officials had a never-ending task of dredging to allow ships to use the port. Shallow-draft boats were able to use the bay throughout the century.

West Pass has what some call an "anchor graveyard" because of all the anchors from ships sunk in the area. One of those anchors can be seen today in front of Wefing's Marina at 252 Water Street in downtown Apalachicola. Some local residents also believe that German U-boats entered the Bay through West Pass during World War II and took distant photographs of Apalachicola.

The State of Florida bought Little St. George Island in 1977 under the Environmentally Endangered Lands Program to protect it from development. The island is now managed by the Florida Department of Natural Resources (DNR), specifically the Division of Recreation and Parks, Bureau of Environmental Land Management. The rangers who patrol the island take shelter from storms in one of the derelict houses the early settlers left behind, a building known today as the Marshall House Field Station. The facility is also used by visiting scouts and educational groups. Although not much of the building remains—thanks to the ravages of pillagers—you can still see the six-foot-square chimney in the center of the house. The fireplace has an opening on each of its four sides and a single flue at the top. Each side of the chimney used to open onto a different room.

The path from Government Dock, an eleven-hundred-foot-long pier where visitors land by boat on the bay side, up to the lighthouse on the Gulf side, may become a nature trail for all to enjoy. Nature campgrounds may also be established in the future, one at each end of the island (where the threat of fire would be minimized). Visitors may also find rusted remnants of the past, such as the elevated platform that helicopters used to land on the island without disturbing the dunes when the U.S. Army used the island for maneuvers. Day-trippers do not have to notify the DNR office, but overnight campers need permission from the Apalachicola National Estuarine Research Reserve's visitor center. See Visiting Information for details.

3.

St. George Island

"Welcome to St. George Island: The Uncommon Florida"

—Sign greeting travelers as they cross

the bridge from the mainland

VISITORS TO ST. GEORGE ISLAND MAY WONDER how "uncommon" the Florida island is, especially when they see the homes crowded along the beach, the restricted access to the western end of the island, and the large number of summer visitors cramming the beaches. At least the northeastern end of the island, which has become a state park, will remain undeveloped.

St. George had an unexpected visitor in the summer of 2001: an infant sperm whale that beached itself on the island. After sharks had attacked it and mangled one of its flukes so badly that it could barely swim, the whale managed to make it to the island, where residents found the twelve-foot, 1,128-pound baby and informed authorities. Scientists then transported "Baby George" to the Clearwater Marine Aquarium near Tampa to nurse him back to health. Although Baby George eventually died, he was the longest-lived sperm whale in captivity.

Baby George's fragility brings to mind the status of the

Loggerhead turtles, some weighing as much as three hundred pounds, return to St. George Island each summer to lay their eggs.

island. Unless Franklin County takes extraordinary care, the continuing development of the place will engulf it and make it one more victim to commercialization. Only time will tell, but—except for the state park—it does not look promising.

The residential population of St. George varies between nine hundred and one thousand. Twenty thousand people visit the island at peak periods. More and more houses are being built on the island. Strict rules limit the size of the lots and houses. Mainlanders refer to the narrow structures, which are usually no taller than three stories and no wider than a two-car garage, as "skinny minis." So many have been built that they block the view of the Gulf for those driving along Gorrie Drive. In order to keep the island as beautiful as possible and to protect services from the damage of hurricanes, builders have put the electric power lines and telephone lines underground. However, environmentalists and others are wary of the septic tanks used by many units, which threaten to pollute the bay.

To the north of the island, between it and the mainland, lie two main bodies of water: Apalachicola Bay and St. George Sound. The bay averages six to nine feet in depth, while the sound averages about nine feet. Off the northeastern tip of St. George is East Pass, which connects St. George Sound with the Gulf of Mexico and separates St. George from Dog Island. The pass is about twenty feet deep, about half the depth of West Pass at the northwestern edge of Little St. George Island.

St. George and the other barrier islands are invaluable to the geography of Apalachicola Bay. They keep the Gulf of Mexico from inundating the bay, thus allowing the freshwater of the Apalachicola River to flow into the bay and provide a good balance for the growing of oysters. Besides blunting the enormous force of hurricanes coming in from the Gulf, the location of the islands also allows a build-up of sand dunes and thus the growth of plants such as sea oats, which help prevent erosion.

The shape and area of St. George are constantly changing, as do other barrier islands in the bay, depending on such natural forces as storms, wave energy, sea level, and sediment supply. It is predicted that as global warming increases because of carbon dioxide buildup in the atmosphere, the sea level will rise, which will dramatically affect the barrier islands.

St. George, which lies between Dog Island (to the northeast) and Little St. George Island (to the west), is about twenty miles long and less than one-third of a mile wide, has about 7,340 acres of land that can be developed and about twelve hundred acres of marshland, and is believed to be three to five thousand years old.

Some believe that St. George Island takes its name from the patron saint of the English, who controlled Florida during the period from 1763 to 1783. However, the name of the island appeared as *San Jorge* on early maps, indicating that it may have been named by Spanish explorers and the English merely translated the Spanish name.

St. George Island remained relatively uninhabited for much of the nineteenth century and has been used over the decades for the raising of cattle and other livestock. Wild hogs and goats also roamed the island. Records show that in 1889, one of the owners of St. George swapped his half of the island for fifty cattle that were grazing on it.

In the early 1900s, workers collected turpentine from the island's pine trees, many of which still show the slash lines from that work. In 1916, William Lee Popham, one of the most important developers of Apalachicola Bay, bought the island for thirty thousand dollars and made plans to develop it by selling lots on the island. World War I halted the development of St. George, but it resumed after the war.

Locals liked to make day excursions to the island, especially during the hard times of the Great Depression, when such a trip cost very little. Some entrepreneurs had ideas of raising goats, sheep, and turkey there, but such plans never really worked out. In the late 1930s, when a local entrepreneur who owned St. George Island could not pay his lawyers for successfully defending him against charges of misleading investors, his defense team acquired the island.

During World War II, troops stationed at nearby Camp Johnston trained in amphibious landings and parachute drops on St. George in preparation for overseas duty. The federal government leased the island for $599 a year so that troops could practice their landings there. In 1943, a U.S. bomber on a routine flight from Atlanta to Panama City crashed on St. George, causing the death of the six crew members.

There is easy access to the mainland from St. George, unlike the other three barrier islands in the bay. There is the four-and-a-half-mile-long Bryant Patton Bridge, built in 1965 from Eastpoint and named after the man who represented Franklin County in the Florida Legislature in the 1950s. When officials stopped charging tolls on the bridge in 1992, many island residents were afraid that free access to St. George would attract troublemakers (which did not happen). In 1992, the Department of Transportation took the bridge from the county under the state road program and has maintained it ever since. That same year, officials named the island Florida Rural Community of the Year, a designation that may become less meaningful as more and more development takes place on the island.

In 2003, Bryant Patton Bridge was completely reconstructed, becoming the third longest bridge in Florida. It retained its name, though it is informally known as the St. George Island Bridge. The bridge cost $70 million, took three years to complete, has two twelve-foot-wide travel lanes (one in each direction) and two ten-foot-wide shoulders, and should last a hundred years. The high-level section of the bridge rises seventy-two feet over the navigation channel. The engineering firm that designed the bridge, Sverdrup, used fewer pilings than in other such bridges in order to disturb the bay's oysters as little as possible.

Officials from the Organization for Artificial Reefs (OAR) used parts of the old bridge to create an artificial reef in the Gulf off the island, just as they did in 1989 with debris from the old John Gorrie Bridge. Thus the existence of at least two artificial reefs: the Apalachicola Reef, located 10.7 nautical miles south-southeast of Bob Sikes Cut (Loran C location: 14217.0 and 46414.0), and the Franklin County Reef, located five nautical miles north-northeast of the Apalachicola

Reef (Loran C location: 14256.0 and 46431.0).

About four miles east of the causeway is the Dr. Julian G. Bruce/St. George Island State Park, which consists of almost two thousand acres and nine miles of undeveloped beaches and dunes. The State of Florida acquired land for the park in 1963, two years before the building of the bridge that has made the island very accessible. The name of the park honors Dr. Bruce, who was a local dentist for fifty years, Franklin County Commission Chairman for twenty-two years, organizer of the Apalachicola Chamber of Commerce, past president of the local Rotary Club, and a conservationist instrumental in establishing the park.

The park was used in the filming of *Little Sweetheart* (1989), starring John Hurt, Karen Young, and Barbara Bosson. Visitors to the park can camp in the campground, hike the trails and boardwalks, swim, sunbathe, use the boat ramps, and fish in the Gulf or bay (with a saltwater fishing license). Four-wheel-drive vehicles are necessary if visitors want to drive to the very end of the island.

A plaque at the park tells about William Augustus Bowles (also known erroneously as Billy Bowlegs, which was the name of three different Seminole chiefs), a white, self-styled leader of the Creek-Cherokee Native Americans, who was shipwrecked when the British schooner *Fox* ran aground in a 1799 storm. Bowles had planned on trading munitions and supplies, which were lost in the shipwreck, to help his Native American allies against the Spanish stronghold at Fort San Marcos. After the wreck, Bowles failed to unite his forces to stop the Spanish and, later, the American control of the area. He was captured in 1803, and died in a Cuban prison two years later. His constant harassment of the Spanish for almost two decades prevented them from maintaining complete military control of Florida.

Students from Florida State University's Underwater Archaeology Program have continued searching, so far unsuccessfully, for the wreck site of the *Fox*, which may be lost because of the slow migration of the barrier island over the site. Marsh Island, which is on the bay side of St. George Island State Park, may be covering remnants of the sunken ship.

Giant loggerhead turtles, some weighing as much as three hundred pounds, return to St. George's shores each summer to lay their eggs. As many as three thousand baby loggerheads hatch on the island each summer, but natural predators consume many of them. Because the turtles are drawn away from the water by lights, residents usually dim or block their house lights when the hatchlings are making their way to the ocean. Also, between May and October, volunteers survey nests, mark them for protection, monitor the nests daily to evaluate their contents and the success of hatchlings, and educate visitors about the sea turtles and the need to protect them.

Among the animals you can find in and around St. George are ghost crabs, raccoons, salt-marsh snakes, and diamondback terrapin. There is also a wide variety of bird species, including the osprey, snowy plover, black skimmer, least tern, and willet, as well as many different kinds of birds that stop on the island on their migrations to and from the north in the fall and spring. The colorful orange, white, and black monarch butterflies also migrate through the island on their way to and from Mexico.

Nick's Hole, a bayside inlet which borders the west side of the island's airstrip, is another important environmental site. In 1993, the state bought forty-eight acres around Nick's Hole, which is considered the third most productive drainage system in the Apalachicola area after the Apalachicola River and the East Bay marshes.

St. George Island has been home to a few writers, among them Forrest Carter and Charles W. Koburger Jr. Carter is the author of *Gone to Texas* (1973), on which the 1976 Clint Eastwood movie *The Outlaw Josey Wales,* is based; *Josey Wales* (1976); *Education of Little Tree* (1976), and *Watch for Me on the Mountain* (1978). Retired Coast Guard Captain Charles W. Koburger Jr. is the author of sixteen books on maritime issues, his most recent one being *The Central Powers in the Adriatic, 1914–1918.*

Each year, on the first Saturday of March, the island hosts the Charity Chili Cook-off and Auction, claimed to be the largest National Chili Society–sanctioned regional chili cook-off, as a fundraiser for the island's volunteer fire department and first responders' unit. With the money raised by this event, the department has bought modern firefighting equipment, which has helped prevent serious fires and has helped reduce fire-insurance premiums.

The threat of hurricanes will always remain, since nothing stands between St. George Island and the open Gulf. So will the threat of developers, who may denude the island of its dunes and protective grasses. While the park on the eastern end will always keep that part in a pristine condition, citizens need to be watchful that builders do not destroy what is left of nature's handiwork on the rest of the island.

4.

Dog Island

"Sugar-white dunes ribbed as if the wind had fingers.

Sea oats rustling in a language all their own. Pine

oaks sculpted by gales into the shape of the southwesterly

breeze—their branches resembling tattered flags frozen

in time, pointing perpetually toward the mainland as if

they were trying to warn or guide us."

—Connie May Fowler, describing

Dog Island in *Remembering Blue*

DOG ISLAND, TO THE NORTHEAST OF ST. GEORGE ISLAND, is a barrier island seven miles long and about a mile wide at its widest. It consists of around two thousand acres, half of which are fresh and saltwater wetlands. It acts as a protector for Carrabelle on the mainland, and at one time it was a quarantine station for ships calling on the town.

Although the island may be about six thousand years old, which is relatively new in terms of geological time, Dog Island, like other barrier islands, including those in Apalachicola Bay, has been moving, or "migrating," as geologists say. As authors Wallace Kaufman and Orrin H. Pilkey, Jr. point out in *The Beaches Are Moving:* "Every day throughout the life of the earth, the wind and the waves have been at work shaping and reshaping the beach, pushing and pulling almost microscopic grains of sand and sometimes boulders larger than cars."

An 1873 hurricane toppled the Dog Island Lighthouse, originally built in 1839, into the sea.

This particular barrier island attracted Native Americans, as indicated by a canoe that archaeologists discovered and dated to over thirteen hundred years ago. On display at Tallahassee's Museum of Florida History, the canoe indicates that Native Americans used the island, or at least the nearby bay, for fishing or oystering.

The first Europeans in the area may have been the survivors of the ill-fated Pánfilo de Narváez expedition of 1528. He and a group of Spanish explorers landed near Tampa Bay, walked north through peninsular Florida, attacked Native Americans along the way, and steadily lost most of their force to battle, disease, and starvation. When they reached present-day St. Marks (south of Tallahassee), they built rafts to escape the area by sea. As they headed west along the shore, they may have seen or visited Dog Island, since it was in their path. They may have referred to it when they wrote: "We sailed seven days among these inlets, in the water waist deep, without signs of anything like the coast. At the end of this time we reached an island near the shore." Only four men from the Narváez expedition eventually made it to Mexico.

Seventeenth-century mapmakers labeled the island *Isles aux chiens* or Dog Island, perhaps because of the wild dogs that, according to legend, French explorers found there, or because the island's topography resembled a crouching dog to someone on a ship.

In 1766, *Le Tigre,* a brigantine full of merchandise on its way from present-day Haiti to New Orleans, was driven north by a fierce storm in the Gulf of Mexico. The ship hit a reef, came apart, and forced the fifteen survivors to swim to Dog Island. The story of the survivors, narrated in the French book *Naufrage et aventures* (1768), is an interesting chapter in the history of Dog Island, although it may have been somewhat exaggerated in terms of all the tribulations faced by the survivors. The Native Americans who found the survivors took six of them to another island, where they robbed them and then left them to die. The six people were Captain La Couture, his wife and son, a man named Viaud, a black slave, and a businessman named Desclau. After the captain and Desclau drowned while paddling a canoe to try to find help, the other four built a raft to try to get to the mainland, but had to leave the captain's son behind when he became sick. The captain's widow, Viaud, and the slave remained alive, but when they were close to starvation, Viaud and the widow killed the slave and ate him. Viaud and the widow then wandered along the coast and may have engaged in a sexual dalliance, but this is only hinted at. Finally, after another ten days of barely surviving, they were discovered and rescued by soldiers from St. Marks Fort at Apalachee. The soldiers also rescued the captain's son.

When the book was first published in France, it scandalized many in Europe who could not believe the cannibalism, starvation, and possible sex among unmarried partners. Auburn University professor Robin Fabel first learned of the story by coming upon a translation of *Naufrage et aventures* while researching the economy of West Florida. Later, he happened upon a letter describing Viad's rescue, which seemed to prove that the events actually took place.

Other shipwrecks have occurred in and near the island. The very severe hurricane of August, 1899, sent large ships crashing onto the sandy beaches. One of those ships was the 554-ton *Vale,* a Norwegian lumber bark that had been involved in the area's lucrative lumber trade since 1896. The *Vale* and eleven other vessels which were offloading ballast and loading pine timber were wrecked, along with the towns of Carrabelle and Apalachicola. Beachwalkers can still see remnants of ships sunk in that hurricane. In 1999, divers from Florida State University's Underwater Archaeology Program found the remains of the *Vale* and partially excavated them. Such shipwreck surveys, done with increasingly sophisticated and technical equipment, will increase the knowledge of the maritime history of the bay.

In 1839, officials built the Dog Island Lighthouse to help vessels navigate into and out of the Bay through East Pass, which is located between Dog and St. George Islands. Workers rebuilt it twice (1843 and 1852) before a hurricane finally destroyed it in 1873. The Crooked River Lighthouse near Carrabelle replaced it in 1895. Remnants of the original Dog Island Lighthouse lie about one hundred meters offshore, more evidence of barrier island migration.

Sponge beds were found in the reefs near Dog Island in the nineteenth century, which brought a short-lived but profitable industry to Apalachicola Bay. Before then, sponges had been harvested elsewhere: in Europe, specifically the Mediterranean Sea, for centuries up until the mid-1800s, and then in the Western hemisphere, particularly the Bahamas and the Florida Keys. Apalachicola Bay seamen used to outfit ships that could be away from port for up to a month. The ships would carry twelve-foot-long rowboats for two-man crews, who would hook the sponges from the bottom, bring them to the ship, and clean and dry them before taking them back to port. Until the local waters were depleted of sponges around 1912, they were a good source of income to the area.

Just as they did on St. George Island during World War II, Allied troops practiced amphibious landings and parachute drops on Dog Island in preparation for overseas duty. A tragic accident occurred in 1945, when ten paratroopers from Fort Benning, Georgia, were blown off course by high winds into East Pass waters and drowned. The heavy equipment they were wearing dragged them to their deaths before rescuers arrived. Today, a plaque at Carrabelle Beach speaks of the importance of Dog Island and Carrabelle Beach in amphibious training for World War II (see chapter 16 for more).

Jeff Lewis, a partner in a flight instruction business in Tallahassee who was flying over the island in 1947, was so impressed with its beauty that he decided to buy it. In 1980, the Nature Conservancy, a private, nonprofit organization that buys lands of environmental value for preservation, acquired thirteen hundred acres of the island and established the Jeff Lewis Wilderness Preserve, which has trails for hiking, bird-watching, and photography.

The Conservancy tried to sell the island to the state or federal government under endangered land acquisition programs, but, when that did not work out, sold it in 1983 to a New York doctor, Thomas Roush, with the understanding that no large-scale development would take place. When that doctor later announced plans to divide much of the land into homesites, the Conservancy bought the land back, although at a lower price than it had originally paid.

The fact that no bridge connects the island to the mainland has helped in its isolation, privacy, and preservation. About two hundred species of birds reside on the island or migrate through it seasonally, and some four hundred species of plants grow there, including a wide variety of wildflowers.

Dog Island is a major spawning ground for blue crabs because of its location, relative security from predators, and topography. Crabs have been known to travel up to three hundred miles in order to spawn near the island. Crabbers have done well there, helping an important Florida industry thrive in the last twenty years.

In 1999, the Organization for Artificial Reefs (OAR) placed over two hundred concrete culverts to form an artificial reef five miles south of Dog Island, in the Gulf. The artificial reef attracts small organisms and the fish that feed on them. The culverts, each about thirty inches in diameter, were stacked on top of each other in five separate piles, forty to a pile, with the piles about 125 feet apart. The money to move the two hundred tons of concrete came from grant funds awarded to Carrabelle through a sportfish restoration program funded by the Department of Natural Resources and the U.S. Fish and Wildlife Service. First the barnacles and small organisms grew on the culverts, attracting bait fish, which in turn attracted big fish like amberjack, cobia, grouper, and king mackerel. The presence of the large fish enhances the annual Big Bend Saltwater Classic Fishing Tournament.

Among the writers who have lived on Dog Island is Celestine Sibley, a columnist for the *Atlanta Journal-Constitution* and the author of such books as *Dear Store: An Affectionate Portrait of Rich's* (1967), *Jincey* (1978), *Children, My Children: A Novel* (1981), and *Ah, Sweet Mystery* (1991). Her mystery, *Straight as an Arrow* (1992), is partially set on the island, as is Mike Stewart's mystery, *Dog Island* (2000). Former Governor Leroy Collins wrote *Forerunners Courageous: Stories of Frontier Florida* (1971) there. Miami poet and artist Laurence Donovan spent time on the island and his book of poems and etchings, *Dog Island* (2003), is the result.

Today, about one hundred houses are on the island, which also has a single dirt road, a small hotel, a grass landing strip, and a private ferry service from Carrabelle (see Visiting Information for details). A sandy road from the island's ferry dock passes near the few homes on the island. Visitors come for the swimming, shell collecting, fishing, and quiet. Only about a dozen or so residents live there all year round.

5.

APALACHICOLA NATIONAL FOREST

"For 5,000 years, it stood as the majesty of the Southland—

a towering pine forest so immense that a traveler could

range 2,000 miles and scarcely walk out of it."

—Frank Stephenson and Bruce Ritchie,

about the territory that once encompassed

Apalachicola National Forest

FLORIDA HAS THREE NATIONAL FORESTS: the Ocala National Forest near Ocala, the Osceola National Forest near Lake City, and the Apalachicola National Forest, which extends across Liberty, Wakulla, and part of Franklin and Leon Counties. Established by the federal government in 1936 and managed today by the U.S. Forest Service, the Apalachicola National Forest is the state's largest at 570,000 acres and only part of what was once a vast stretch of trees which extended from Virginia to Texas across the Deep South. Within it, there is one spring; 2,735 acres of lakes; and six watersheds consisting of one creek (Lost Creek) and five rivers: the Apalachicola, New, Ochlockonee, Sopchoppy, and Wakulla. These rivers and numerous streams in the forest provide a steady freshwater supply to Apalachicola Bay and Ochlockonee Bay, which are well known for their oyster and other shellfish production.

The name Apalachicola is related to that of the local Apalachee Indians, whose name means "the people who live

The Apalachicola National Forest, at 570,000 acres, is the largest national forest in Florida.

on the other side" and who are believed to have lived around the Apalachicola River in the sixteenth and seventeenth centuries. Human beings have inhabited parts of the Florida peninsula for over ten thousand years. Because the barrier islands offshore are too newly formed and freshwater was an important determinant for settlements during the Paleo-Indian Period (10,000 B.C.–7,000 B.C.), it is likely that any Native American settlements that existed during that time were located around the Apalachicola River, although artifacts indicating such settlements have not yet been found.

Archaeologists have found artifacts from the Archaic Period (7,000 B.C.–500 B.C.) which indicate that Native Americans lived in the Apalachicola Valley, hunted small animals, fished, and used fiber and pottery. Toward the end of that period, in what is known as the Deptford Period, they cultivated plants, used sand-tempered ceramics, and lived in villages. Many burial mounds and middens testify to the existence of larger villages as time went on.

The forest harbors many plant species, including cypress, longleaf pine, magnolia, oak, and slash pine. The *Harperocallis flava* or Harper's Beauty is a subspecies of lily that grows nowhere else. Its name honors Roland McMillan Harper (1878–1966), a botanist who studied plant life around Apalachicola. In addition, more than three hundred animal species make their home in the forest, including indigo snakes, gopher tortoises, alligators, bald eagles, ospreys, red-cockaded woodpeckers, snowy egrets, turkeys, squirrels, white-tailed deer, and black bears.

The red-cockaded woodpecker is one of several rare birds found in the forest. The approximately 1,500 woodpeckers living there give Florida the distinction of having the largest group of such birds in the country. Because of logging restrictions in the forest, the birds were able to make a strong comeback so that the Florida Fish and Wildlife Conservation Commission voted unanimously in 2002 to reduce the woodpecker's designation from threatened to "species of special concern." Scientists with the U.S. Forest Service are engaged in a program to nurture the birds in this forest and then transplant the offspring to other national forests throughout the United States.

The forest has been a prime site for scientists to study black bears, which have decreased in number due to the state's rapid development and deforestation. Careful monitoring of the bears in the 1990s by the Fish and Wildlife Conservation Commission, which captured, tagged with radio collars, and released bears into the forest, told scientists about the animals' territory range, seasonal movements, habitat use, and denning traits. Because of the relative scarcity of food in the Apalachicola National Forest, black bears tend to roam more widely there than elsewhere—up to eighty-one square miles for adult males and twenty-five square miles for adult females. Because northwest Florida is much colder than peninsular Florida, the bears in the forest also tend to hibernate for much longer periods than do bears farther south (for example, in the Ocala National Forest)—sometimes up to five months.

The colonization of the land that is now the Apalachicola National Forest began during the time the British controlled Florida (1763–1783). Three Englishmen—William Panton, Thomas Forbes, and John Leslie—set up a trading operation named Panton, Leslie, and Company near St. Augustine, which was part of British East Florida at the time. They acquired a vast amount of land in Florida by befriending Alexander McGillivray, who was half–Native American and half-Scottish and a leader among the Creeks who lived north of the Apalachicola Forest. The trading company sold goods to the Native Americans on credit (though it is not clear whether they fully understood the concept of buying on credit). When the Native Americans could not repay their debts, the company appropriated plots of their land. The company continued to claim this ownership even after Spain retook control of Florida in 1821. The company's holdings eventually became known as the Forbes Purchase and encompassed around 1.3 million acres on the lower Apalachicola River. With the intent to sell the land to incoming white settlers, the company moved its headquarters to Pensacola and established branches throughout the territory, including at Prospect Bluff, the site of the famous Fort Gadsden up the Apalachicola River (see chapter 13). Today, Forbes Island, a very large body of land in the National Forest between

Brothers River and the Apalachicola River just southwest of Fort Gadsden, is a reminder of how important the Forbes Purchase was to the development of Franklin County.

When the United States acquired Florida from Spain in 1821, the legality of the land acquisition by the company became a burning issue that the U.S. Supreme Court eventually resolved in 1835 by declaring in favor of the company. At that point, the company, which had become the Apalachicola Land Company, was free to sell lands with clear titles to the incoming settlers. Many adventurers and settlers moved into the area along the Apalachicola River and around the Apalachicola Bay before Florida became a state in 1845.

During the Great Depression, the U.S. government established many national forests, including the Apalachicola National Forest in 1936, in order to preserve the sites, restock and replant them, and manage them for all Americans. Today, the Forest Service allows carefully regulated lumbering in the forest. Visitors may see workers cutting down previously marked trees, removing the tops, "skidding" the trees to waiting trucks, and then hauling them away to sawmills or paper mills to be converted into manageable wood or paper. Workers then replant tree seedlings to replace the trees that were taken out.

Wakulla, Franklin, Liberty, and Leon Counties have worked out a plan with the federal government to receive payments from the U.S. Forest Service in lieu of the taxes they would earn if environmental regulations did not curtail tree cutting. For example, the Franklin County government and school board will each receive thirty-two thousand dollars a year from the federal government from 2003 through at least 2009.

The forest, if Franklin County officials agree, may become part of the Florida Department of Transportation's Florida Scenic Highways project. This is neither a land-acquisition program nor a road-construction program, but a designation program for a specific corridor possessing special "intrinsic resources" which can be scenic, natural, recreational, cultural, archeological, historical, or combinations thereof. The proposed Big Bend Scenic Byway would be a 248-mile path through existing roads in Wakulla, Franklin, Liberty, and

Leon counties, the longest scenic byway in Florida. It would bring in more ecologically minded visitors, but also take advantage of the natural beauty that so often gets neglected in the rush to pave over much of the state to make highways, parking lots, and condominiums.

Apalachicola National Forest offers extensive opportunities for fishermen, hunters, campers, boaters, picnickers, and other visitors. The Florida Trail in the forest has been certified as a Florida National Scenic Trail. And the whole trail has been designated as part of the Florida Statewide Greenways and Trail System. Today, hikers in the forest can often find relics of the people that once inhabited the forest, including arrowheads, spear points, and pieces of pottery, often near the surface. Finders should carefully keep records of what they find and the location, so that trained archaeologists can better identify the artifacts.

While the economy of Franklin County relies on the Gulf of Mexico and Apalachicola Bay for much of its income—especially from fishing, clamming, and oystering—some of the people on the mainland depend on other sources. One of them is bee culture, an industry that produces around 350,000 pounds of tupelo honey each year and brings income to many local beekeepers. Tupelo honey is a remarkably light honey that never becomes granular and seems to be the only form of honey that diabetics can eat because of its high levulose content and low dextrose ratio. The swampy lands in the lower Apalachicola basin may have the largest natural stand of tupelo in the world. The locally filmed 1997 movie *Ulee's Gold,* starring Peter Fonda, features tupelo honey and tells the story of a beekeeper in northern Florida who has to deal with his jailed son's former partners in crime.

One unusual practice you may see in and near the forest is "grunting," or "fiddling," by which people drive stakes into the moist soil, rub a piece of heavy iron along the top of the stake to produce underground vibrations (which have a "grunting" sound), and collect the many worms that come to the surface to escape the sound. Fishermen use the worms in the many waterways of the forest. The town of Caryville to the northwest of Franklin County began holding an annual worm-fiddling contest in 1974 to go along with its self-imposed title of Worm-Fiddling Capital of Florida.

The Apalachicola National Forest is one of the jewels of wild Florida. Worm-fiddling, bear-tagging, and tupelo-gathering are just some of the unusual activities you can find along this Forgotten Coast.

6.

APALACHICOLA RIVER

"If the effort [to bar the Apalachicola River as a navigation waterway] is successful, it will end a chapter of the Apalachicola where the river provided a transportation link for Florida and points north for almost 200 years."
—Stanley Kirkland, "The Steamboat Era on the Apalachicola, Chattahoochee and Flint rivers"

IN 1982, GERALD GROW IN HIS "FLORIDA IN 2001" report, stated that "just before the turn of the 21st century, population growth in Atlanta drained so much of the Chattahoochee River—the headwaters of the Apalachicola— that the Apalachicola began to dry up, the estuary turned salty, productivity plummeted, the productive annual flooding of the flood plain forest declined and, for most purposes, the river started to die." That statement, made over twenty years ago, did not come to pass—but it might have, and it still might, if Georgia, Alabama, and Florida fail to agree about how to solve the many conflicting claims on the river. But what a disaster the death of the river would be!

Every day, sixteen billion gallons of freshwater flow down the Apalachicola River into Apalachicola Bay, mixing with the saltwater coming in from the Gulf and providing a rich estuarine system for many species of marine life. Destroying the river or diverting too much of its water to Atlanta or Alabama could bring economic ruin for the Floridians who depend on the oyster and fish-

Steamboats used to deliver passengers and cargoes up and down the Apalachicola River.

ing industries in Apalachicola Bay.

The Apalachicola River is the twenty-first in magnitude of all the rivers of the lower forty-eight states and the largest one in Florida, with a mean annual flow of twenty-five thousand cubic feet per second. From time to time, that flow increases as engineers release significantly higher amounts of water from Lake Seminole at the Jim Woodruff Dam at the Georgia border in order to try to flush out the red tide that occasionally plagues the bay, kills fish, and shuts down the collection of oysters.

The river is formed from the joining of the Chattahoochee and Flint Rivers. Together, the rivers drain almost twenty thousand acres in Alabama, Georgia, and Florida. The Apalachicola River is about 106 miles long from its beginning at Jim Woodruff Dam near Chattahoochee, Florida, due north of Apalachicola Bay, to the bay. The river, which scientists estimate formed around twenty-five million years ago, in the Miocene Age, falls about forty feet from the Woodruff Dam to the bay.

The Chipola River joins the Apalachicola River twenty-five miles above the bay, and together they form a wide flood plain extending from two to almost five miles across. The flood plain has many cypress, tupelo, and hardwood trees. At seventy-one miles long and covering about 122,000 acres, it is the largest one of its kind in Florida. It includes another twenty-two thousand acres if you add in the non-forested area, marshes, and open water. Some sixty different species of trees are found in this area. In addition, the Apalachicola River system has one of the largest tracts of bottomland hardwoods in the Southeast, second only to the Mississippi River system.

The flood season, if there is one in any particular year, will occur from January through April; the river's flow decreases during the fall months of September through November. Every decade or so, massive floods inundate the upper parts of the river in Georgia and Alabama, forcing animals like the black bear, white-tailed deer, and wild turkey to move to higher ground.

The Apalachicola has some of the most spectacular

scenery in all of Florida, partly because it has so few homes along its length, especially immediately south of the Florida-Georgia border. The ravines there are so steep that lumbering companies have found it too expensive to take out the trees from the slopes. What the shade and cool temperatures of the river's banks have provided is a place where flora has grown since the last ice age. Two of the rarest evergreens in the world, the Florida yew and the Florida torreya, live along the river. The upper basin of the river has more endangered plant species than any comparably sized area in Florida. In addition, the area around the Apalachicola hosts the highest density of reptiles and amphibians in the United States and Canada, as well as the greatest diversity of freshwater fish species in Florida.

Native Americans, probably of the Creek tribes, lived along the river in what came to be known as Bay City, a large area which is on present-day 12th Street in Apalachicola. Mussel-shell middens and artifacts found there point to the presence of a large number of Native Americans. As more archaeology digs proceed, scientists may find more pottery and remains that will tell us more about the lifestyle of the people who lived there.

In the nineteenth century, as merchants and traders looked to establish ports on Florida's Gulf coast, some chose Apalachicola rather than other harbors and bays that would allow ships to dock. They did so because of the presence of the Apalachicola River, which allowed access to potentially good markets in Alabama and Georgia. Later, during the Seminole Indian wars of the eighteenth century, the Seminoles used the river to elude army troops, who found the region's mosquitoes, dense vegetation, and lack of nearby roads difficult to handle.

During the Civil War, Confederates used ship-building facilities farther up the river in Columbus, Georgia, as well as other facilities along the river, to construct ironclads and gunboats. Salt-making, a common activity around Apalachicola in the first few years of the Civil War, was eventually shut down by raiding Union troops, but not before local workers supplied the Confederacy with a much-needed material for preserving food.

Around 1950 the Army Corps of Engineers began building a dozen reservoirs and dams, including the Jim Woodruff Dam (completed in 1957), along the Chattahoochee–Flint–Apalachicola river system. The U.S. Congress had authorized the Corps of Engineers in 1946 to maintain a navigation channel one hundred feet wide and nine feet deep as part of an effort to industrialize the South. Because roads and rail facilities were not adequate at the time, and because barges were considered the most economical way to move large cargo over long distances, engineers convinced Congress to dredge the Apalachicola, Flint, and Chattahoochee Rivers. As roads and railroads were built in the second half of the twentieth century, the need for dredging the rivers lessened, but proponents of the channels have been able to convince Congress to keep funding the dredging.

Many ecologists predicted, accurately, that this would hurt the river and everything in it. The Army Corps of Engineers seemed to ignore warnings from environmentalists and fish experts, as more dams were built on the rivers which prevented fish from going upstream to spawn. While such dams provided lakes for recreation, the damage they did to the fish populations may be permanent unless accommodations are made for them, such as creating waterways that bypass the dams and allow the fish to complete the journeys they have been making for thousands of years. For some fish species, the damage has been so great that today the rivers must be stocked if these fish are to remain in the river system.

The striped bass has been severely affected by the dams. Another fish of special concern is the Gulf sturgeon, which dates back 250 million years and is thus one of the oldest living species of fish in the world today. The Gulf sturgeon is found in the Gulf of Mexico and a few Southern rivers, including the Apalachicola. It used to provide many fishermen with a good business, as the fish were prized for their meat and caviar, but water pollution has killed off many of them. To protect the fish, in 2001 the Fifth U.S. Court of Appeals in New Orleans forbade the Army Corps of Engineers from dredging the areas where the Gulf sturgeon lay their eggs.

In 2002, the American River Organization named the Apalachicola River one of the nation's most endangered because of the many dredging and flow manipulations it has endured. Barge traffic on the river has decreased significantly from 229 barge trips a year in 1989, to 47 in 1999, to only 30 in 2000, but Congress continues to fund the dredging. In 2001, Congress allocated eight million dollars to the dredging operations, while it spent some five million to remove the large piles of sand from earlier dredging. The Corps has buried more than a quarter of the river's banks under giant mounds of sand dredged from the river. Those mounds smother vegetation and prevent water from entering the river's side channels and sloughs.

Because the river flows through parts of Alabama and Georgia before reaching Florida, what the first two states do to the river affects Florida directly. People in all three states need it for drinking water, fishing, hydroelectric power, boating, recreation, and irrigation. Irrigation by farms north of Florida is a serious problem because the amount of water used for this purpose tends to be highest in the fall season, when the flow of the river is at its lowest. Increased drainage of the water away from its main flow decreases the amount of freshwater that flows into Apalachicola Bay, thus upsetting the delicate balance between freshwater and saltwater that is essential to the thriving oyster-gathering business in the bay.

For the past ten years, officials from the three states have been arguing over how to allocate the resources of the Apalachicola–Chattahoochee–Flint basin. The parties involved have different goals for the basin. Florida wants to maintain the flow that has provided such a rich oyster-growing area in Apalachicola. Georgia wants more water for Atlanta, irrigation for farms in the southwestern part of the state, and deep reservoirs for recreational use and for emergency use during droughts. Alabama wants water for its cities, industries, and navigation. Finally, the federal government wants enough water to protect endangered species along the river and meet its standards of water quality, flood control, and other federal issues. The difficulties are legion.

Florida and Alabama argue that Georgia takes too much

water from the river basin in order to meet the needs of Atlanta's huge metropolis. Compounding the problem is the fact that Atlanta has old, badly maintained sewage pipes whose breakup would endanger the rivers south of there. Florida and Georgia contend that Alabama takes too much water for irrigation purposes. Alabama and Georgia, in turn, argue that Florida's water demands for Apalachicola's oyster business hurt their chances for using the rivers. The Chattahoochee River, which has its headwaters about eighty-five miles north of Atlanta and which joins the Flint in Lake Seminole just north of Chattahoochee, Florida, to form the Apalachicola River, has been named one of the ten most endangered rivers in the United States by the American River Organization, primarily because of the pollution from Georgia and the demands placed on the river by the three contiguous states.

Since 1997, the states have been trying to work out a solution among themselves without getting the courts involved. Two of the main issues being debated are water quality and the amount of water that will flow through each state. The states are wrestling on how to regulate the water flow during drought years and how much water should flow down into the bay. In 2002, the three states reached an initial agreement that would help protect the Apalachicola from deterioration. The states agreed to set minimum flows of the river at Chattahoochee at five thousand cubic feet per second, which is the minimum needed for endangered mussels to survive; to double the river flow at Chattahoochee to ten thousand cubic feet per second in March and April each year, when the federal reservoirs upstream have more water; to extend the agreement until 2050 and force the burgeoning Atlanta region to seek new water supplies; and to allow the release of water from reservoirs to allow barges to move upstream only in emergency circumstances. The governors of Florida, Alabama, and Georgia signed a Memorandum of Understanding in 2003, but there are still some issues that need to be ironed out, for example, whether Atlanta's willingness to pay a lot more for the use of more water would violate previous court rulings that did not allow that. The hope is that the states will establish an Apalachicola–Chattahoochee–Flint [ACF] River Basin Compact, a long-term agreement that would meet the needs of all three states and would be the first of its kind in the United States.

Apalachicola Bay and River Keeper, Inc. (ABARK), an affiliate of the International Water Keeper 6 Alliance, is one of several concerned citizen groups involved in the preservation of the Apalachicola. Its many activities include a river cleanup, a program to protect nesting turtles on St. George Island from the disturbing effects of electrical lighting near the shore, and newsletters to inform the public about dangers to the river.

The stretch of almost one hundred square miles from the town of Wewahitchka down to Apalachicola is known as the Apalachicola River Wildlife and Environmental Area (WEA). It is currently preserved by the state as a CARL (Conservation and Recreation Land) area, which are lands the state has acquired in the last two decades and whose natural habitat it tries to preserve as much as possible. Squirrel hunters and bass fishermen use it throughout the year, but state officials preserve the area by enforcing certain rules, for example, by restricting the number and kinds of fish that can be caught, or setting certain times of the year as the times when hunters can shoot certain animals.

The varied terrain along the river may be used as a training ground for this country's special operations forces and law enforcement personnel to replace similar, much more expensive programs in Puerto Rico and Panama. A proposal presented to the Apalachee Regional Planning Council in 2001 noted that the river, islands, and swamps, together with the long runways at Apalachicola's airport would make an ideal location for such training. Such a program would bring in much income to the county as forty-three thousand Army Rangers, Navy Seals, and Air Force Combat Patrol Teams train there each year. The project will certainly receive opposition from those who want to protect the river from more encroachment. If the Gulf Marine Assistance Center is approved, officials will hire about thirty of the local deer hunters and worm grunters (see chapter five for more about grunting) to act as a mock opposition force that could ambush and capture military trainees and hold them as hostages. (Can you imagine a trainee on the telephone: "Dad, you won't believe this, but a worm grunter captured me here in Apalachicola.")

Also, in 2003, the Florida Department of Environmental Protection helped establish a one-hundred-mile corridor linking the Apalachicola National Forest with Eglin Air Force Base in order to protect a variety of ecologically sensitive natural communities including estuarine tidal marshes and floodplain swamps. Such a corridor also protects the quality of water necessary for oyster harvesting.

On the river, north of the town of Apalachicola, is Scipio Creek Marina and Mooring Basin. The basin was established by the U.S. Congress River and Harbor Act of 1954, and has been home to a number of commercial boats. The marina began operating in the nineteenth century, when lumber companies would float their logs down the river before shipping them elsewhere. Later, crabbers and shrimpers used the site. St. Vincent National Wildlife Preserve is headquartered at the marina; the preserve has a small museum with exhibits about St. Vincent Island including a Sambar deer's antler and dioramas depicting the island's marshes and animals. The city-owned commercial marina at the end of Market Street has been used to harbor small boats, even mid-size shrimp boats, while the larger boats used the wharf downtown.

The future of the Apalachicola River is unclear. If Alabama, Georgia, and Florida are really determined to keep the strength of the river and not dilute it with the siphoning off of water for Atlanta's drinking needs and Alabama's irrigation requirements, if the U.S. Army Corps of Engineers can be convinced to stop dredging the river and piling up huge mounds of destructive sand, if the river is relieved from its use as a waterway for large barges and is allowed to revert to its natural state, and if up-river pollution can be stopped before it contaminates Apalachicola Bay, then the river should last for many more centuries and continue to serve the many people who depend on it.

7.

APALACHICOLA NATIONAL ESTUARINE RESEARCH RESERVE

"With thousands of miles of coastline, and no point more than sixty miles from sea water, Florida has always depended on maritime trade."
—Roger C. Smith, *An Atlas of Maritime Florida*

THE PRESENT AND FUTURE RICHNESS OF FLORIDA'S maritime trade depends on many factors, one of which is how Floridians take care of their estuaries. An estuary is a semi-enclosed area, such as a bay or lagoon, in which salty ocean water meets fresh water. It might be at the wide lower course of a river where its current meets the tides, or where an arm of the sea that extends inland joins the mouth of a river. There, fresh water mixes with salt water, providing a unique place between the land and the sea where many organisms can thrive. The wide variety of species that live in estuaries have to be able to adapt to changing conditions such as dry times because of changing tides, or extreme temperatures, which may freeze shallow estuarine waters in the winter or create very hot environments in the middle of summer.

The qualities of the estuary change according to the water's salinity, tides, sunlight, and temperatures. What is essential to maintaining a healthy estuary is a balance between salt and fresh water. That balance can be upset by

A boardwalk into the Apalachicola National Estuarine Sanctuary allows visitors to see a wide variety of wildlife.

hurricanes and storms that thrust the ocean or Gulf into the bay, by causeways that impede the flow of saltwater through the daily tides, by dams or river diversions that hinder the flow of fresh water and their many nutrients into the bay, and by droughts which can cut down on the amount of fresh water available. And while the estuary may recover from such events, the sea life that dies cannot always be easily replaced.

With their mixture of fresh and salt water, with their constantly changing tides and temperatures, and with their many different marine organisms, estuaries cleanse the water of excessive nutrients and other chemicals that people and factories have introduced into the water system. Ninety-five percent of Florida's fish, crustaceans, and shellfish spend part of their lives in estuaries, usually when the sea life is young and developing. Crustaceans and fish usually spawn or breed offshore, and the resulting eggs change into larvae, which tides and currents transport into estuaries, where they can hide from predators in the marshes and grasses. Such places also provide roosting and nesting areas for many birds. In the case of Apalachicola Bay, the destruction of estuaries and the subsequent pollution of ocean waters would harm the important oyster and fishing industries and the economy of Franklin County and Florida.

Apalachicola Bay is one of several estuarine areas in Florida's Panhandle (there are others at Pensacola Bay, Choctawhatchee Bay, St. Andrew Bay, and Apalachee Bay). In 1979, the Office of Coastal Zone Management established the Apalachicola National Estuarine Sanctuary, known today as the Apalachicola National Estuarine Research Reserve or ANERR. The ANERR is part of a system to manage healthy estuaries across the country as sites for long-term research and education. Of twenty-six such sites in the country, the state of Florida has three—more than any other state. The one at Apalachicola Bay is the largest in the contiguous United States at approximately 247,000 acres (of which 135,000 are under water). It is second only to Kachemak Bay Reserve in Alaska. The boundaries of the ANERR, which extend fifty-two miles, include the Apalachicola River, St. Vincent Sound, St. George Sound, and other barrier islands.

Florida State University and the Florida Sea Grant College do research in the reserve. ANERR headquarters have laboratories, educational facilities, and administration offices.

The establishment of this reserve has allowed the lower Apalachicola Valley to become a natural field laboratory where scientists can monitor and study natural systems and where students and the general public can learn about an estuary in a natural setting. The estuary here is part of Apalachicola Bay, which itself is unusual because of the influence of five very different physiographic areas: the Appalachian mountains, the Piedmont, the Atlantic coastal plain, the Gulf of Mexico coastal plain, and peninsular Florida. The size of the bay allows a wide diversity of aquatic life, from sea grasses and swampland to oysters and clams to crabs and fish. The advantage of establishing such a reserve in the bay is that the area includes many different habitats (fresh water, sea water, brackish water, marshes, bayous, river flood plain, barrier islands, submerged vegetation, and oyster bars) that can rarely be found in one place in this country. The reserve has outreach education programs, off-site educational presentations, a quarterly newsletter *(The Oystercatcher),* and boat trips to such places as Fort Gadsden up the Apalachicola River and to Little St. George Island (including overnight stays on the island) for groups of interested individuals.

More than thirteen hundred species of plants are found in the area. Three dozen of those species are threatened or endangered varieties. One of the trees in the area, the black tupelo gum tree, grows in the swamps and produces the excellent tupelo honey. The basin also has over one hundred species of fish, including the endangered Atlantic sturgeon, bluestripe shiner, and Suwannee bass. Almost three hundred bird species make their habitat in the basin, including two dozen that are threatened or endangered. The basin is also one of the most diverse sites for amphibians and reptiles in North America.

The establishment of the Apalachicola estuary as a National Estuarine Sanctuary in 1979 necessitated that Alabama, Georgia, and Florida work together to formulate policies all could live with. The purpose of establishing the estuary was not to block development, but to ensure that development does not harm the ecosystem. Interested officials are trying to preserve the productivity of the bay without halting all development of the area's resources. Because the flow of fresh water from the Apalachicola River into the bay is such an important ingredient in the health of the sanctuary (and therefore, of the oyster and fishing industries), officials are very concerned about the talks among the three states concerning the regulation of the river's flow. (See chapter six for more about those negotiations.)

Florida's coastal sites are under great pressure from developers who want to build high-rises and homes for the state's burgeoning population, many of whom come to enjoy the state's renowned beaches and waters. Almost eighty percent of the people in the state live in coastal areas. Dredge-and-fill operations for waterfront communities destroy a lot of the sea life along the coast, including in the estuaries.

The Apalachicola River is under pressure as well. Because commercial interests use the river to barge products to and from Georgia and Alabama, over the years some have proposed to dredge and straighten parts of the river to facilitate that traffic. Strong arguments from knowledgeable scientists about the effects of such actions on the bay have discouraged these projects. Considering the possible negative consequences makes clear how interdependent all the concerned parties are, including citizens, businesspeople, policymakers, environmentalists, as well as the many shrimpers, oystermen, and fishermen who depend on a healthy bay. Only the purchase and protection of environmentally sensitive estuarine areas by the state and federal governments or by such organizations as the National Audubon Society and the Nature Conservancy can guarantee that the lands will be saved for future generations.

Part of the natural run-off from the Apalachicola River is detritus, debris from rotting vegetation upstream that is swept into the bay, where it provides the basic ingredients for the food chain. The barrier islands toward the Gulf hem in the freshwater in the bay long enough for the detritus to settle to the bottom. The continued flow of a large quantity of fresh water from the Apalachicola River is essential to the good health of the estuary.

While that runoff can be useful, other runoffs are dangerous to estuaries, for example, the many fertilizers, herbicides, and pesticides used on farms, as well as the auto and industrial emissions found in the more developed parts of the state. But in trying to prevent these problems, different industries are often at loggerheads. The aerial spraying of insecticides to control mosquitoes, for instance, is sometimes necessary, but the chemicals that remain in the environment and are washed into the waters can have harmful effects. An example is the insecticide fenthion causing the death of juvenile shrimp, which spend the early part of their life in estuaries; fortunately, very few Florida counties use fenthion today.

Because Florida established the Apalachicola National Estuarine Research Reserve before developers had a chance to do irreparable harm to the land around the bay, scientists have high hopes that the sanctuary will last into the foreseeable future. In 1983, Florida State University biology professor Robert J. Livingston finished a twelve-year study of the Apalachicola Bay system and produced *Resource Atlas of the Apalachicola Estuary,* a work meant to guide county officials on the best ways of preserving the area's water system without completely eliminating all development. Because the bay is one of more than forty sites in the Florida Aquatic Preserve Program, some of its lands have been set aside forever for preservation and conservation. In addition, the area is protected under state designations as Aquatic Preserve, Outstanding Florida Waters, and Class II Shellfish Harvesting Waters. A portion of it is designated as an Area of Critical State Concern. It has also been designated as an EPA Gulf of Mexico Ecological Management Site and as a Biosphere Reserve by the United Nations UNESCO.

Overall, the future of the estuary seems bright. Apalachicola residents and visitors celebrate National Estuaries Day each fall. The Estuarine Walk near Scipio Creek on Seventh Street in Apalachicola allows participants to take guided tours around the "touch tanks" and exhibits of estuarine life. Visitors can also take a boat ride on the reserve's research vessel, including a trip up Scipio Creek to take a close look at the natural habitats and species living in the reserve. A public that is more aware of the value of estuaries will help to see that estuary protection laws are enforced and new laws enacted. The introduction of environmental education in our schools will also help make future generations aware of how valuable estuaries are for everyone.

Florida's estuaries and long coast are monitored by several organizations. For example, the Florida Fish and Wildlife Conservation Commission maintains the Florida Marine Research Institute in St. Petersburg to monitor and study the changing Florida coastline, which is under constant pressure from developers who want to dredge and fill in estuaries to build more condominiums and houses. The thousands of mangroves destroyed in places like Biscayne Bay, Sarasota Bay, and Tampa Bay have led to a decline in the fish and bird life found there. Current state and federal laws, enforced by the Florida Department of Environmental Regulation and U.S. Army Corps of Engineers, no longer permit the wholesale destruction of such coastal wetlands. It will take such close monitoring to make sure the Apalachicola National Estuarine Research Reserve stays healthy and continues performing its valuable service.

8.

COTTON

"Apalachicola consisted twelve months ago of
about one hundred shanties, confusedly spread over
a surface of a quarter of a mile square, but now has
numerous regular streets and a continuous front along
the river, of three-story brick houses with granite
casements, three quarters of a mile long."

—*The Apalachicola Gazette*, 1837

THE COTTON WAREHOUSE THAT YOU CAN STILL find in downtown Apalachicola hearkens back to a time before the
Civil War when Apalachicola was the state's largest cotton
port and the third largest port on the Gulf after New Orleans
and Mobile. Remnants of other brick warehouses remain, but
most are long gone as a result of storms, fires, decay, or to
make way for other buildings. Apalachicola's dramatic
change of status as a cotton port after the war indicates how
perilous it can be to depend on one crop, especially when it is
not grown in your own territory.

Cotton played a major role in the early history of
Apalachicola Bay. In fact, an early name for the town of
Apalachicola was "Cotton Town" or "Cottonton" because of
all the cotton that was shipped through there. The name later
became West Point for the geographical position of the town
in reference to the river, but Florida's Legislative Council
changed it to Apalachicola in 1831 under pressure from the

Apalachicola was the state's largest cotton port before the Civil War.

local residents, who felt that "West Point" was an "uninspired" name.

Cotton was very important to the little town of Apalachicola even though farmers did not grow much in the area. Instead, Apalachicola became a conduit for shippers to move the cotton down the river, to the town, and out to waiting ships. The land in Franklin County, in fact, has never been very good for agriculture, and the offshore islands proved unsuitable for the growing of sea cotton, which had made the Georgia sea islands profitable. Thus, the economic boost that cotton brought to Apalachicola was precarious, since it depended on a variety of external factors—mainly on whether the growers would continue to ship cotton down the river and to the bay.

Rivermen used flatboats to ship cotton down the Apalachicola River after the United States took control of Florida from Spain in 1821. Two years later, with the appointment of Charles Jenkins as the first customs collector at the bay and the building of his residence near the mouth of the river, the little settlement began to grow and take on importance. In 1836, fifty thousand bales of cotton were shipped through Apalachicola.

By 1837, the little town was doing so well in the cotton trade that some forty-three three-story brick warehouses lined the waterfront, ready to take in cotton from up the river, compress it, and ship it out to different parts of the United States and Europe. The warehouses earned the town the nickname "The Brick City" or "The City of Granite Fronts." By 1840, some 130,000 bales of cotton were being shipped out of the town each year, bringing in between six and eight million dollars annually and making Apalachicola the third largest cotton port in the Gulf of Mexico. In addition to cotton, a huge amount of products was imported into the town for shipment up the river.

Rivalry over the cotton trade led to bad feelings between Apalachicola and the town of St. Joseph, which was the scene of Florida's Constitutional Convention in 1838. Two years before, people had established St. Joseph in an attempt to break the hold of the Apalachicola Land Company (which owned much of the land in and around Apalachicola since 1835) and ship cotton to other ports. In order to bypass Apalachicola, officials in nearby towns built one of Florida's first railroads. It ran from Iola (a once-bustling town that used to lie on the shores of the Apalachicola's west bank, but which no longer exists) to St. Joseph.

Storms and disease would often interfere with the area's commerce. Huge storms in 1837, 1839, and 1844, coupled with a yellow fever epidemic in 1841, effectively destroyed the town of St. Joseph, which would not revive until the 1900s. The cotton shipping industry had helped Apalachicola's population grow from around 150 in 1828 to around 2,000 in 1838, although many residents lived elsewhere in the summer months, when fever, humidity, and heat made living there unbearable and less commerce moved on the river. But yellow fever also threatened Apalachicola in the 1840s, especially during the so-called "fever months" of August through October of 1840 and 1841, during which the population of the town shrank below a hundred. Officials used the non-fever months of December through June to do most of the cotton shipping.

When the Civil War struck, Apalachicola was the first Florida port to be blockaded by Union ships, an indication of how highly the North held the cotton-exporting town. That blockade was so successful that it curtailed much of the shipping to and from the port, as well as the ferrying of supplies up the Apalachicola River to inland towns—despite the fact that Union ships were too big to go up the river to provide them with supplies. The bay area also had a number of salt-producing facilities that provided the means for Confederate armies to preserve meats and other perishable foodstuffs. These operations were eventually shut down by Union forces.

Even though the silting up of parts of the bay prevented the large Union vessels from maneuvering easily, Confederate and Union forces took turns occupying the port. No battles of importance took place in the area, but there were two significant smaller engagements. In 1862, ten miles away from Apalachicola, near Crooked River, Confederate soldiers of the Beauregard Rangers attacked a boat carrying twenty-one

Union soldiers from a blockading ship; seventeen of the Union soldiers were captured or wounded, but none of the Confederate troops suffered casualties. The following year, Union troops went twenty-three miles up the Apalachicola River, confiscated the schooner *Fashion* at Scott Creek, captured several soldiers and fifty bales of cotton, and took them all back to the blockading vessels in the bay. When the war ended, troops of the 82nd United States Colored Infantry and the 161st New York Volunteer Infantry occupied Apalachicola. The town soon returned to normalcy, and the shipment of cotton resumed.

Worse than the effects of the war on the cotton trade of Apalachicola was the effect of railroads on commerce routes. The river, with its north-to-south traffic, became less important in the transportation of cotton as the railroads emphasized east-to-west routes. Savannah, Georgia, grew in importance because of its Atlantic location and the fact that railroads could take the cotton there. Because Apalachicola served as an exporting site for cotton grown upriver, especially in Alabama and Georgia, the town depended on those sources for its shipping trade. If those sources began shipping their cotton by rail to the east coast, the town at the mouth of the Apalachicola River would suffer the consequences— which is what happened.

If the little town had depended solely on income from cotton for its livelihood, it might have withered and died. Instead, it had a resource just offshore in Apalachicola Bay that saved it and allowed it to prosper into the twenty-first century.

9.

OYSTERS

"The best investment on earth is the earth itself."

—William Popham, Apalachicola oyster entrepreneur

A N APALACHICOLA RADIO STATION CALLS ITSELF Oyster Radio, a very appropriate name considering that Franklin County oystermen harvest ninety percent of Florida's and ten percent of the nation's oyster crop. That livelihood is under different kinds of threats every year, whether from development pollution or water contamination by Atlanta's sewage making its way into the Apalachicola River and the bay, or from natural threats from the Gulf of Mexico, such as red tides or hurricanes. Oystermen worry that the bay will become like Chesapeake Bay, which used to have many oysters before pollution damaged it severely; or like Tampa Bay, whose once-thriving seafood industry was greatly damaged by uncontrolled growth; or like Boston Harbor, which had raw sewage pumped into it for many years and has been severely harmed, perhaps irreparably.

The history of oystering in Apalachicola Bay goes back a long way. Archaeologists who have examined Native

Harvesting oysters in the bay has always involved hard work and long hours.

American shellmounds along the coast of Apalachicola Bay have concluded that the Apalachees who inhabited this area ate oysters and discarded the empty shells in mounds that reached considerable heights. Those first residents may have inhabited the Apalachicola Bay area for as long as ten thousand years, until diseases and wars brought by European explorers wiped them out.

The newly arrived whites in the nineteenth century did not take advantage of the oysters other than for local consumption, primarily because they grew cotton, which they hoped would make them rich. In the end, the area did not prove to be good for cotton growing, and the town began to depend instead on the shipping of cotton from points farther north. When railroads began bypassing the area—for example, by going directly to Bainbridge, Georgia, from other points—Apalachicola lost importance as a cotton-shipping port, and residents of Apalachicola Bay began to rely on the little oyster for their livelihood.

They were successful enough in this activity that they were shipping oysters out in barrels before the Civil War. But the turmoil of the war interfered with the harvesting. As a result, oysters were able to grow and develop relatively undisturbed for a few years. By the 1870s, the oystermen were back in business, sending out barrels of oysters and making a good living. In the 1880s, state law gave exclusive rights to plant and harvest oysters in designated waters to those who requested the appropriate permissions from county authorities. The oystermen realized that the different locations of the oyster beds in Apalachicola Bay produced different-tasting oysters, depending on the amount of salinity and other factors. That led to competition for the best oyster beds.

At the beginning of the twentieth century, the lack of railroad connections and the inability to refrigerate oysters for shipments elsewhere greatly curtailed the oyster industry. The local oystermen formed the Oystermen's Protective Association to try to establish uniform prices and have more control of their business, but that did not work out as successfully as they had hoped. Various get-rich-quick schemes involving oysters brought in investors, but in the end many of them lost money. The most enterprising man was William "Oyster King" Popham (1885–1953), who convinced four thousand Northerners to invest in oyster beds in Apalachicola Bay that would supposedly bring in over $1,000 a month in income. His newspaper, the *Oyster Farm News*, convinced many to join his Oyster Growers Cooperative Association and invest in the schemes. Popham succeeded in promoting the oyster industry around Apalachicola Bay in the early 1920s and introduced some successful oyster-planting procedures, but legal troubles landed him in jail for two years (1926–1928), and the Great Depression further curtailed his ambitious plans for the bay.

Oysters thrive in Apalachicola for a variety of reasons. The bay has the perfect mixture of salt and fresh water for oysters to develop. The shallowness of the bay, the temperature of the water, the protection afforded by the barrier islands, the influx of the Apalachicola River, and the many nutrients washed down into the bay from the river turn the bay into a nutrient-rich body of water with low salinity, an ideal environment for oysters, shrimp, and many kinds of fish. Scientists estimate that about forty percent of the Apalachicola Bay water area is suitable for growing oysters. While oyster bars are found throughout the bay, the major concentrations are on either side of the Bryant Patton Bridge from East Point to St. George Island, around Goose Island off St. George Island, between St. Vincent and Little St. George Islands, and off the northern shore of St. Vincent Island.

Different methods have been used over the years to retrieve oysters from the bay. They include tonging, in which a man on a boat would use long, double-handled rakes with double prongs to extract the oysters from the seabed; hogging, in which pickers could walk over the oyster beds at low tide and pick up the oysters by hand; or dredging, in which a dredge or wire basket would be dragged over the sea bottom to pry loose the oysters—a method that often destroyed oyster beds and was subsequently outlawed. In recent years, the Florida Marine Fisheries Commission has allowed the limited use of oyster dredges, but with strict rules and careful enforcement. Many local oystermen opposed the introduction of oyster dredges for fear that such dredges would become widespread.

Today, the favored method of extraction is to use nine-foot-long tongs to reach the oysters on the bottom of the bay. The oyster skiffs used in Apalachicola Bay have been adapted to the conditions of the area; they have flat bottoms to ease navigation in the shallow bay and are powered by outboard motors to reduce disturbance to the oyster beds. Husbands and wives can be found working together on the oyster boats in Apalachicola Bay. Some two to three hundred families depend on the oyster industry for a livelihood. That figure includes the 770 people who were given oyster-harvesting licenses in 2003 and the many restaurant people who cooked and served oysters.

A relatively new method of growing oysters, aquaculture, was introduced in the 1980s when then-Governor Bob Martinez approved a $450,000 project to teach it to local oystermen. Aquaculture is a way of cultivating oysters that involves putting small oysters in porous plastic bags, attaching the bags to pipe frames, submerging the pipes in the bay, and cultivating them over time. The project was initiated after hurricanes in 1985 and a drought in 1988 resulted in poor oyster harvests. Aquaculture gave a boost to the industry as it changed oystermen from hunters to farmers.

The major natural threats to the local oyster business are disease, predation, and competition from other organisms. The balance of the water's salinity is essential: if the salinity is high, saltwater predators such as the southern oyster drill and the stone crab are more likely to enter the bay from the Gulf. On the other hand, low salinity can stress and kill the oysters. Droughts, which cause less water to flow into the Apalachicola River and thus into the bay, cause the salinity in the bay to rise. Hurricanes, which can ravage the sand bars of the bay, are another major threat. For example, Hurricane Elena, which hit the bay in September, 1985, destroyed most of the oysters in the eastern part of the bay around Cat Bay and East Hole.

The area for productive oyster beds has decreased dramatically in the last century due to development, pollution, and overfishing. Two major changes were the building of Sikes Cut between St. George and Little St. George Islands (which increased the salinity of the bay by letting in more Gulf water) and the construction of the Jim Woodruff Dam near the Florida-Georgia border (which altered the natural flow of the Apalachicola River). Both structures also allowed more parasites into the bay, which harmed the oyster beds. The beds are so sensitive that even short periods of low salinity in the bay can hurt them.

The Department of Natural Resources has helped the oyster business in various ways. For example, it has allowed oystermen to move live oysters from closed areas, which are unproductive for oyster growing or susceptible to red tide infestations, to approved locations, which are more productive and free of the red tide. It has also placed dead oyster shells in the sea bottom in order to create new oyster bars, which are often ready for harvesting within two years of their creation. When such reefs reach maturity, they can produce as many as four hundred bushels of oysters per acre. Artificial reefs have been very successful in the harvesting of oysters, producing as much as half of the bay's total. Scientists have built over 750 acres of reefs in the bay since 1949.

Partly to protect the oyster industry and preserve jobs in the area, the Florida Legislature passed the Apalachicola Bay Protection Act of 1985, more popularly known as "1202" because that was the number of the House bill. The bill was meant to upgrade Franklin County's sewage system and therefore stop the seeping of sewage from coastal communities that was threatening the health of the bay. The bill also gave the State Department of Community Affairs (DCA) the power to control development in the county, which many opposed because they wanted local control over development decisions. Even those opposed to the Apalachicola Bay Protection Act of 1985 would probably admit that the oyster industry is strong today, although it faces constant threats from nature.

From time to time, officials have to close the harvesting of oysters in the bay because of pollution caused by effluent from local sewage treatment plants or faulty septic tanks, bad sewage lines, or even storm-water runoff. The isolated cases of infectious hepatitis from the eating of oysters from the bay have caused unwanted publicity and put excessive fear into the minds of consumers. However, regulatory actions have maintained a consistently healthy crop of oysters from the bay and have therefore alleviated the worries that consumers might have about eating oysters.

Since 1914, Apalachicola has celebrated Oyster Day. Beginning in 1915, a local personage was selected King Retsyo ("oyster" spelled backwards) to preside over festivities that included airplane flights by W.S. Luckey, an early aviator who probably made the first takeoff and landing in the history of the town. Today, the annual seafood festival, which takes place in the fall, attracts thousands of visitors each year. It includes the Blessing of the Fleet ceremonies, in which ministers of various local churches bless the local boats involved in the oyster business; an oyster-eating contest; and the crowning of Miss Florida Seafood.

Dr. Robert Livingston, director of the Center for Aquatic Research and Resource Management located at Florida State University, spent twelve years studying Apalachicola Bay and provided data to aid in the formation of the Apalachicola National Estuarine Research Reserve. A lot of his work dealt with the factors influencing the oyster. He and other scientists could point to Chesapeake Bay, the largest estuary in the United States and once a major producer of oysters, as an example of a site where uncontrolled development damaged the bay's environment and the oyster industry, perhaps irretrievably. He made it clear that if development was not planned carefully in Apalachicola Bay, which is one-eighth the size of Chesapeake Bay, the decline would be very rapid. Dr. Livingston's importance to the oyster industry led to his being selected King Retsyo at the Florida Seafood Festival in 1981.

The fate of the oyster industry depends on how future generations handle the ongoing problems afflicting the Apalachicola River, development on the barrier islands (especially St. George), and the control of natural debilitating forces such as the red tide. When engineers designed the new bridge to St. George Island, they were careful to relocate oysters from the construction site to Cat Point area near Eastpoint. If such care is always taken in the future, consumers a hundred years from now will still be able to order oysters from Apalachicola Bay.

10.

SHRIMP, FISH,
AND OTHER SEAFOOD

"Looking down river from Georgia, you see three rivers.

Looking upstream from Apalachicola, you see one river, and

that's a much more accurate perspective."

—Woody Miley, former manager of the

Apalachicola National Estuarine Research Reserve

O N THE FIRST SATURDAY OF NOVEMBER EACH YEAR, over fifty thousand people descend on Apalachicola for its annual Florida Seafood Festival, which was begun modestly in 1963 and now can claim to being the oldest maritime festival in the state. Every other weekend, another seven thousand people show up to tour the town and partake of its culinary delights, especially its seafood.

While Apalachicola Bay is best known for its rich oyster harvest, the harvest of seafood in general has been an important business there. Residents of Franklin County have been chiefly employed in shrimping, fishing, clamming, and, in past years, sponging. Up until recently, between sixty and eighty-five percent of the citizens of Franklin County have made a living from the seafood industry, which contributes more than eleven million dollars a year to the local economy

Shrimp boats still use the waterfront in Apalachicola to dock and store their catch.

and eventually generates over seventy million dollars a year by the time all of the seafood reaches restaurant tables.

Apalachicola Bay has the ideal location, climate, temperature, and water flow for cultivating seafood. Most important is its location: the bay is near the Gulf of Mexico, which provides forty-two percent of all the seafood harvested in U.S. waters. The bay is also part of a protected national estuary, and ninety-five percent of all seafood that is commercially harvested spend part of their life in an estuarine system.

The area has a climate that is milder in the summer than Georgia's in the summer because of the proximity of the Gulf of Mexico and also much colder than peninsular Florida's in the winter because of its latitude. Rainfall averages about fifty-six inches a year, most of it occurring in the summer and fall. Hurricanes also strike during that time period, and they affect the rainfall totals as well as the configuration of the islands. In the last century, twelve minor hurricanes (with winds between 74 and 110 mph) and four major hurricanes (with winds greater than 110 mph) have hit within fifty miles of the bay. Tidal variations, however, are slight; the normal tide range in Apalachicola Bay is only one to two feet, primarily because the continental shelf slopes gently off the northern and western shores of Florida.

The average temperature of the bay is very conducive to seafood harvesting, ranging between 54.4° Fahrenheit in January to 81.4° Fahrenheit in July and August. The occasional freezes only last for a few days, maximum. The winds usually vary in direction: cold, dry fronts from Canada bring north to northeasterly winds in the fall and winter; warm, moist, southerly winds from the Gulf of Mexico come in the spring and summer.

Water movement in the bay is from east to west, with the saline water from the Gulf of Mexico entering through St. George Sound, flowing west, mixing with water in East Bay and Apalachicola Bay, and exiting into the Gulf through Sikes Cut, West Pass, and Indian Pass. The Apalachicola River discharges about twenty-five thousand cubic feet of water per second into the bay, with its strongest effect in the immediate vicinity of its mouth—although it does affect the salinity of the whole bay as it mixes with water from the Gulf. The volume of discharge of fresh water into the bay from the Apalachicola River is determined more by rainfall in Alabama and Georgia than in Florida.

Transportation has been a key factor in the success of the seafood industries in Apalachicola. In the nineteenth century, Apalachicola lacked an extensive railroad system to transport the bay's seafood products elsewhere. The Apalachicola Northern Railroad was completed in 1907, running north to Gadsden County, where it could connect with east-west lines. The advent of the refrigerated truck in the twentieth century and the building of good roads in Franklin County have been instrumental to its modern success.

The potential for shrimping in Apalachicola Bay was not realized until the early nineteenth century, when local fishermen stopped discarding the shrimp they caught in their nets and began deliberately gathering it from shallow-water boats in the bay. The Bay City Packing Company, begun around 1915, shipped canned shrimp to markets elsewhere. When fishermen discovered that brown and pink shrimp were active at night, they began working at nighttime to catch the fresh shrimp.

One can still see, between Water and Commerce streets on Avenue E (Highway 98) in the town of Apalachicola, the *Venezelos,* an old shrimp boat that recalls the days when shrimping brought more income to the town than it does today, since cheaper imports have usurped some of Apalachicola's market. Shrimp boats and fishing boats still use Apalachicola as headquarters and store their catch in refrigerated seafood buildings along the dock. Those boats represent the maritime heritage that has made Apalachicola important in the history of Florida. Today the historic town is still a working fishing village despite the fact that far more people work in non-fishing industries, especially service and tourism.

Each year, when the conditions are right, shrimpers harvest up to six million pounds of shrimp from Apalachicola Bay, making it one of the best areas in Florida for shrimping. Several species of penaeid shrimp thrive in the bay, including white (*Penaeus setiferus*), pink (*Penaeus duorarum*), and brown (*Penaeus aztecus*). The most abundant species in the bay is the white shrimp.

Each species has its own spawning season and preferred spawning ground depth. Adult shrimp migrate offshore in the Gulf of Mexico, where they spawn and the eggs hatch before currents transport the larvae to the estuary. The larvae develop into juveniles in the tidal marshes, which provide low salinity, protection from predators, and abundant food. As the juveniles develop into sub-adults, they move to other parts of the estuary. When the temperature of the water decreases, they migrate offshore to the adult grounds to spawn. Because the shrimp migrate into the Gulf when they reach maturity, it is difficult to estimate the amount of juvenile shrimp in the bay at any given time.

Besides oysters and shrimp, the bay also harbors blue crabs, which can migrate as far as three hundred miles in order to get to Apalachicola Bay to spawn. Fishermen can also find many species of fish in the bay, including the bay anchovy, striped mullet, flounder, speckled sea trout, red fish, croaker, spot, and sand sea trout. Mullet is a major commercial fish that has brought in as much as one hundred thousand dollars a year to Florida's economy. Eighty-five species of freshwater fish and over one hundred species of saltwater fish are found in the bay.

One of the reasons fishing is so good in the Gulf south of the bay is that officials have constructed artificial reefs from such objects as the remains of the old Gorrie Bridge, which was dismantled in 1988 when a new bridge was built. There are about thirty artificial reefs in the bay, made up of things such as a sunken ship, concrete culverts, and concrete reef balls. The oldest and biggest is the *Empire Mica* ship, which was sunk in 1942. Although it is difficult to determine exactly how much the artificial reefs have improved local fishing, the strength of the fishing industry along this coast suggests that they are very effective.

For years, many thought that natural reefs were not present in the continental slope off the Florida coast in the Panhandle. But unexpectedly, scientists have discovered a natural reef seventy miles south-southwest of Apalachicola Bay. It is a coral-topped reef that extends over three hundred square miles in depths of eighteen to thirty fathoms (108–180 feet). The reef provides a fishing ground full of red snapper and grouper.

Clamming is another activity that takes place in Apalachicola Bay. The state's clam-farming industry, begun in the 1980s around Indian River Lagoon on the east coast of Florida, now includes 350 clam-producing farms around the state and produces over 140 million clams with a value of twenty-one million dollars a year. In 2001, the Florida governor and cabinet approved the introduction of clam-farming on one hundred acres of state-owned, submerged land along the northern shore of Alligator Harbor, east of Dog Island.

Clams are useful not only for their food value, but also for their ability to restore and maintain water quality by filtering water and removing suspended soils from the ocean. The clams, which can filter up to one hundred gallons of sea water a day and have helped clean canals in Brevard, Charlotte, and Lee counties, should do the same for Apalachicola Bay.

Sponge-gathering used to be a large business in the bay. Until the nineteenth century, most sponges came from the Mediterranean, but divers discovered them off Florida in the 1840s, especially off the Florida Keys. Later in that century, spongers from Greece, who came to Florida specifically to work in the sponge-gathering business after its decline in Greece, worked out of Tarpon Springs and eventually Apalachicola. In the last part of the nineteenth century and the first part of the twentieth, divers retrieved sponges off Apalachicola and Dog Island.

Dinghies operating from larger vessels would use a spotter to peer beneath the water with a glass-bottomed wooden bucket and then use a pronged pole to hook the sponges and bring them up to the boat. The spongers would take the sponges back to the larger vessel, which would take them to port when enough had been gathered. The peak year of the sponge industry in Apalachicola was 1901, when twenty thousand dollars' worth of the product was brought in. That was a decent amount of money for the local sponge collectors, but their hopes of doing even better did not come to pass. As sponge beds were depleted, the spongers went elsewhere, and the local fishermen resorted to the more profitable activities of fishing and oystering. The Sponge Exchange is an old brick building in downtown. It is one of two buildings remaining in the city as vestiges of that age.

Over the years, entrepreneurs have tried new ventures with yet other kinds of sea products. For example, in the early 1940s, locals established a factory for processing crabmeat and for processing menhaden, a saltwater fish used for making oil and fertilizer. Such ventures succeeded for a while, but today, the importation of cheap seafood from abroad, the reluctance of youngsters to go into the difficult and seasonal seafood business, and the vagaries of weather have hurt such businesses.

Problems abound in the state's seafood industry, including natural threats, pollution, and overfishing. Natural threats include hurricanes and tropical storms, whose winds can dramatically affect the tidal pattern of the relatively shallow bay. Another occasional threat is the so-called "red tide," a naturally occurring, higher-than-normal concentration of the microscopic algae *Karenia brevis* (formerly *Gymnodinium breve*). This organism produces a toxin that can paralyze fish and will sometimes lead to large numbers of dead fish washing up on Gulf beaches. Pollution dangers can arise from the construction of the many new homes being built in the area, especially on the barrier islands. The threat of pollution from commercial fishing boats has been lessened by the regulation that all such boats must have portable lavatories on board. Shrimping by large trawlers may eventually be outlawed because trawling tends to wreck the bottom of the bay, and trawling fishermen often throw a lot of what they collect back into the water, although it is dead by then.

Overfishing led to the passing of a controversial amendment to the state constitution limiting the use of fishing nets in 1995. Many who had earned a good living by catching such species as amberjack, grouper, snapper, and many other finfish have gone into other businesses. The result has been a huge reduction in the annual income of the region. One hope of many to survive difficult economic times is to become more involved in tourism, which shows signs of becoming a promising industry in Franklin County.

Some worry that Apalachicola Bay will become like Key West and Tarpon Springs, places where seafood once reigned, but where pollution and overfishing killed the industry. Local officials and residents are hopeful that they can learn from the mistakes of others and keep their bay productive for generations to come.

11.

LOGGING AND SAWMILLS

"Timber is the very life-blood of Apalachicola—its past support and future stay, at least until this vast undeveloped territory gets more capital and people to till the soil and start diversified industries."

—*North & South* magazine, June, 1909

IF YOU LOOKED AT THE TIMBER RESOURCES AVAILABLE in Franklin County in 1900, you would have to agree with the above assessment. One writer estimated that five billion feet of longleaf yellow pine stood in the area. Tributary streams of the Apalachicola River could help bring much of this resource to the small town at the foot of the river to be sent on its way in waiting ships. So what happened? Why didn't the timber resources of Franklin County bring in great wealth to the county? And why did Carrabelle have more success with the timber industry than Apalachicola did?

The area just north of Apalachicola and Carrabelle has had an abundance of trees for thousands of years, but—despite all those trees—other factors conspired to thwart the timber industry. Those factors include high transportation costs, a clogged river, relatively few skilled workers, and the absence of a deep-water port at the mouth of the Apalachicola.

The growing, cutting, and transporting of timber have provided many jobs to the residents of Franklin County.

Even if the natural problems had been solved by digging a deep port and unclogging the river on a regular basis, the lack of skilled labor prevented the full utilization of timber. When, for example, the congregation of Apalachicola's Trinity Episcopal Church wanted to build a church in 1838, they had to go to New York to commission workers to build a church and ship it down to Apalachicola. The shipping of cotton through Apalachicola and the harvesting of oysters and shellfish in the bay, as well as fishing in the Gulf, took up much of the region's manpower. Then, when the Union blockaded the bay during the Civil War, ships could not take lumber out of the area.

After the Civil War, when conditions seemed right for an economic upturn of the county through the shipment of cotton, railroads bypassed Apalachicola and sent the profitable cotton by rail to eastern cities such as Savannah, Georgia, forcing the Florida town once again to struggle for its livelihood. Without cotton to sustain them, Apalachicola and Carrabelle turned to the nearby abundant forests for help. The 1870s saw the area—especially around Carrabelle—begin to develop its timber resources, build sawmills, and ship out railroad crossties from the many cypress logs cut in the area. Lumbering increased traffic on the Apalachicola River by some seventy percent at the end of the nineteenth century.

One place where you can see remnants of the logging industry and sawmills is at Bay City Lodge out on 12th Street in Apalachicola. The Bay City Saw Mill Company and others along the river operated into the second quarter of the twentieth century. Visitors can see remnants of a large loading dock in the river, the cement foundations of a steam-driven log-skidder, part of a narrow-gauge rail line, and a sawmill.

You can see a different type of remnant of the lumber industry in Apalachicola near the shrimp boat marina. Because the logging mills were often on well-situated property near bodies of water, their location is now valuable for beautiful homes. The former site of an abandoned cypress mill is where an enterprising woman, Jane Doerfer, moved a nineteenth-century house from another part of town and refurbished it to such an extent that *House Beautiful* featured it in 1995.

If in the nineteenth century local officials had been able to bring in a railroad to serve Apalachicola and Carrabelle and transport the harvestable lumber, or to dig a deep-water port at Apalachicola or Carrabelle and allow ships to dock close to the land, the economic fortunes of Franklin County would have been different. But neither of the above occurred.

If Apalachicola had succeeded in obtaining funds for a railroad, it would have been able to ship its lumber by rail, but the funds never materialized. When it became clear that Florida officials would not fund a railroad to Apalachicola, the town considered, in desperation, joining others in the Florida Panhandle in seceding from the state. The idea was that by joining Alabama, Apalachicola might get a railroad. But that did not come to pass. Apalachicola and Carrabelle could have also prospered from the Cross-Florida Barge Canal, but that project ended when, among other things, environmentalists pointed out how much harm it would cause south Florida.

Alternately, if local officials in Apalachicola had succeeded in convincing federal authorities to deepen West Pass, whose relatively shallow depth would not permit ships drawing more than eleven feet of water, the town might have done better in the lumber trade, especially after the federal government used funds to clear the Apalachicola River of snags and to deepen and widen the channel entrance near the town in the 1870s.

Carrabelle, however, fared better in its bid to profit from the lumber industry. The swamps around the town seemed to have a limitless supply of timber, especially ash, cottonwood, cypress, longleaf yellow pine, poplar, sweet gum, and tupelo gum. When the Carrabelle, Tallahassee, and Georgia Railroad Company completed tracks to Carrabelle at the urging of Carrabelle's leaders, especially Oliver Hudson Kelley, lumber companies such as the Franklin County Lumber Company were able to ship out lumber and provide Carrabelle's citizens with good jobs. Also, the channel near the town was much deeper than that near Apalachicola, which enabled deep-draft boats to ferry lumber out to ships near East Pass, which was also better suited for large ships than West Pass near

Apalachicola, between St. Vincent and St. George Islands.

The lumber companies around Carrabelle accommodated the wishes of buyers around the world. Some wanted only square-sawed logs, which would be placed in the ships' holds in one piece. When workers unloaded those logs at ports around the world, local millers would cut them to local standards and uses. Other buyers wanted hewn logs, railroad ties, shingles—all of which the local mills did their best to produce in order to accommodate their clientele.

Lumber companies did more than cut down trees and ship them out. They also kept the trees in place and harvested products like turpentine and rosin. Around the year 1900, distilleries on New River, near Carrabelle, employed woodsmen to cut into pine trees, fasten cups onto the trees, and harvest the gum or sap that would flow from the trees into the cups. The men would dip out the product and take it to the still for processing. Clay pots, later tin pots, nailed to the tree, replaced the large cavities that were formerly used. The gum would be dumped into huge copper distillery pots that wood fires would heat and which—with the addition of water—would produce turpentine or rosin, depending on the market demand for each. It took eight barrels of gum to produce two barrels of turpentine or four barrels of rosin. The turpentine or turpentine sap from the pine trees was used for making pitch to repair boats and paint thinner, while rosin was used for varnishes. Today, pulp mills manufacture these products with more modern methods.

Companies outside the region owned some of the land and lumber companies; one example is the Cypress Lumber Company, which was owned by Northern investors. James N. Coombs, who was relatively wealthy at the beginning of the twentieth century, owned several lumber mills. Coombs, a New Englander from Maine, came to the Apalachicola area after the Civil War and established two large mills: one up at the Bluff and one at Carrabelle. The wealth he made from lumber enabled him to build one of the most elegant homes standing in Apalachicola today, the Coombs House Inn at 80 Sixth Street. His heavy involvement in the timber industry made him turn down the Republican Party's nomination for governor in 1900. Two other important local lumber companies were the Loxley Lumber Company and the Carrabelle Land and Lumber Company.

The area around Carrabelle prospered until the end of World War I, when the decreasing demand for timber and naval products forced mills like the Franklin County Lumber Company to close for good. In addition, the lack of reforesting caused the depleted land to lose its value and forced many businesses to close and people to move elsewhere or engage in more profitable and steady businesses such as oystering and fishing. Today, one company engaged in reforestation around Carrabelle is the Buckeye Cellulose Corporation. This company plants nineteen thousand seedlings each year in Franklin County, with a survival rate of about eighty-five percent. Its goal is to be able to harvest trees in the area for many years to come.

When the lumber companies left the area in the twentieth century in search of better areas, many of their camps remained abandoned. One such camp, Harbeson City on Crooked River, three miles north of Carrabelle, was transformed during World War II into a mock German village called "Shickelgruber Haven," where American troops training at Camp Gordon Johnston learned street-fighting techniques such as door-to-door fighting.

Today, the St. Joe Company owns nearly 940,000 acres in Florida, most of it in northwest Florida, with seventy thousand acres of that in Franklin County. The company also owns about eight acres along the coast of Franklin County, which it may develop, especially as more and more residents or vacationers move in. This giant company will continue to have influence in the future of the area and may build summer resorts along the Gulf to take advantage of the insatiable demand for such vacation sites by Floridians and others.

Except for its few towns and St. George Island, most of the land in Franklin County is used for forestry and conservation, the latter mostly in lands owned by the federal or state governments. Over ninety percent of the county consists of forests, land used for conservation purposes, or submerged land under rivers, lakes, streams, or the bay. Such vast stretches of forest give a rural flavor to Franklin County, provide hunting and fishing opportunities, and purify the air of the Panhandle.

12.

STEAMBOATS

"Sailing ships had brought in some of the early settlers. However, these ships could not navigate the inland waterways. After steam began to be used for propulsion in the 1800s, steamboats started to supplant sailing vessels."

—From *Steamboats in 19th Century Florida,* a publication of the Florida Heritage Education Program

ONCE MOST NATIVE AMERICANS WERE REMOVED from Georgia, Alabama, and Florida—except for those like the Seminoles, who fled into inaccessible swamps—trade opened up for settlers in the nineteenth century. In the 1820s, more and more people were moving into Florida and settling in its fertile areas, including areas along rivers like the Apalachicola. Because the area still had few good roads, the people along the rivers depended on boats, especially steamboats, to bring them products and mail and to carry other settlers.

Geography has played a big part in Apalachicola's history and commerce. The small town was founded because of its proximity to the Gulf, bay, and river, and so the town's residents naturally came to depend on water transportation. Plus, some four hundred square miles of river and swamp surrounded the town, and an immense forest reached from near the Alabama border to the Gulf of Mexico. The swamp harbored hostile Native Americans and runaway slaves up

Travel by steamboat was the only feasible way to reach Apalachicola in the eighteenth and nineteenth centuries.

until the 1800s, making overland trips dangerous, and the offshore islands had their share of pirates and outlaws.

Other than the small, competing settlement of St. Joseph thirty miles west of Apalachicola, no other sizable settlement was anywhere near the small town. Pensacola, over 150 miles to the west, could be reached by boat, but that settlement was controlled by the Spanish until 1821.

Long before the Gorrie Bridge was built in 1935, a ferry boat connected Apalachicola to Carrabelle and parts farther east and north. Even so, those with good foresight realized that the railroad was key to the success of the area and began encouraging politicians and businessmen through newspaper editorials and town meetings to build a line to Carrabelle and also to Apalachicola. Such an undertaking, however, would not occur until the beginning of the twentieth century, and would only reach Carrabelle. Meanwhile, the merchants and other residents of Franklin County knew they had to depend on boats to travel.

Boat traffic was the only feasible way to travel to and from Apalachicola in the eighteenth and nineteenth centuries. The distance from Apalachicola up the river to what became Chattahoochee at the northern tip of Florida was over one hundred miles, a distance that steamers could travel fairly easily, as they went up even farther to Alabama and Georgia. Farmers, planters, and merchants up and down the Apalachicola River, as well as along the Flint and Chattahoochee, depended on steamboats for getting products into and out of the territory. Some of the enterprising merchants from Apalachicola, in fact, owned warehouses farther up the river, for example in the growing Florida town of Chattahoochee on the border with Georgia.

When the steamboat *Fanny* reached Columbus, Georgia, in the spring of 1828, the town of Apalachicola realized that much of its economic success depended on steamboats. Soon, fifteen steamboats plied the Apalachicola River, ferrying cotton down to Apalachicola. By 1830, more than five thousand bales of cotton were shipped south. All along the Apalachicola River were dozens of river landings from which farmers could ship their produce. The steamboats would take all kinds of supplies upriver and then return with loads of cotton, timber, tobacco, and other farm products.

But Apalachicola soon had a major rival to the west: St. Joseph, with its deep-water port. Established in 1829 with the intention of diverting the flow of cotton from Apalachicola and, later, hosting the First Constitutional Convention of the Territory of Florida (1838–1839), St. Joseph seemed destined to surpass little Apalachicola, and thus began a bitter rivalry between the two settlements. That rivalry tilted in the newer town's favor in 1839, when workers built a railroad to transport cotton to St. Joseph from Iola, which was on the banks of the Apalachicola River. Eventually, that would change dramatically and Apalachicola's importance would be restored when hurricanes and a yellow-fever epidemic destroyed St. Joseph around 1841.

If Apalachicola could not get a railroad, at least it could prosper with steamboats. Around 1830, more than 130 steamers used the Apalachicola River, sixty-four of which listed Apalachicola as their home port. Workers in the port built eight of the steamers that plied the river, but most of them came from plants in Pittsburgh, Pennsylvania; Cincinnati, Ohio; and Elizabeth, Pennsylvania. The steamboats carried passengers and freight, including cotton, corn, rice, tobacco, lumber, turpentine, animal skins, and food. When the steamers reached Apalachicola Bay, workers would transfer the exports to schooners and frigates, which would take the goods to distant ports.

Just before the Civil War, more than fourteen million dollars worth of goods had been shipped by steamboat through Apalachicola. When Union patrol boats effectively blockaded the town during the war (1861–1865), that amount fell to zero. After the war, traffic resumed on the river, with the shipment of timber becoming increasingly important. By the late 1890s, some 750 trips were made up and down the river by vessels bringing more than fifty-one million board feet of lumber to Apalachicola. That, combined with the town's three oyster-canning factories, which could produce fifty thousand cans of oysters each day, and the seafood industry, which was producing six thousand barrels of salted fish and crates of sponges, brought in almost four million dollars of revenue to the area.

The type of boat used on the river was determined by the river itself. The typical steamer in the 1830s weighed about 130 tons, had a draft of thirty-five inches when fully loaded, and could carry one thousand bales of cotton and fifty passengers. Larger vessels, like the 148-ton *Steubenville,* could carry seven hundred bales of cotton or eleven hundred barrels of flour. Most of the steamers were side-wheelers rather than stern-wheelers, because the heavy weight of the latter's boilers and stern wheel caused too much stress on the vessel's hull, especially in a swift, shallow river like the Apalachicola. Also, sailing up against the current demanded the greater control of the side-wheelers.

River pilots had to be very careful of the twists and turns of the river, of the fallen trees and shallow points, and of anything on board that might cause a fire. Steamboats like the *Fanny,* an eighty-eight-ton steamer that stretched eighty-nine feet long and seventeen feet wide with a six-foot-deep hold, had to proceed with caution on the river, since fallen trees and sandbars provided constant threats. At Fort Gadsden, up the river from Apalachicola, visitors can see the remains of the steamer *Irvington,* which was carrying cotton in 1838 when it burned and sank four miles upstream.

While a six-foot-deep channel remained in the river for much of the year, unwary pilots ran the serious danger of running aground on submerged sandbars or hitting concealed rocks and trees. The vessels normally ran only during daylight hours, when the dangers were bad enough; trying to navigate the river at night was asking for trouble. Many steamboats burned or sank in the river, some of them so fast that passengers drowned.

One way the river was made more accessible to steamboats was by dredging, an operation that has been done many times over the years, but which has received more and more opposition in recent years because the scant use of the river by large boats does not justify the environmental damage caused by huge sand piles along the banks.

In the end, Apalachicola lost most of its cotton trade

because of factors that were out of the hands of the locals. The river needed constant dredging, an expensive operation particularly in the Reconstruction period, when money was tight. Periodic droughts lowered the level of the river. The railroads diverted traffic from the town, funneling it off to Savannah and other, more conveniently located ports. After being the Gulf's third largest port in the 1850s, Apalachicola's status declined dramatically after the Civil War.

Hopes for some kind of a revival of the cotton trade arose in the early twentieth century when Charles Duff and his company built the Apalachicola Northern Railroad in 1907. The line's seventy miles of track stretched to Gadsden County, where it connected with east-to-west railroads. Two years later, the line connected to St. Andrew Bay, where Port St. Joe was established on the former site of the long-gone St. Joseph. Apalachicola also had a connection to the Georgia, Florida, and Alabama Railroad in 1909 through a ferry connection to Carrabelle. That line gave access to Tallahassee and Georgia and to ports north of there. The Georgia, Florida, and Alabama Railroad also owned the Lanark Village to the east of Carrabelle, where the railroad officials had built a fashionable resort meant to attract visitors and residents from other states at the beginning of the twentieth century (see chapter 14).

Steamboats continued using the Apalachicola River in the early 1900s, delivering passengers and cargo to towns along the way. One favorite destination was Bainbridge, Georgia, where two railroads met to take cargo and passengers to and from the steamboats. The Great Depression of the early 1930s, along with the increased use of buses, trains, and cars, finally doomed steamboat traffic on the Apalachicola. The last steamboat to use the river, the *J.W. Callahan, Jr.,* went into receivership in 1932 and was dismantled. That particular vessel had been built in Apalachicola in 1915 and headquartered in Bainbridge. Like other such wood-burning steamers, it would stop along the river to load wood for its furnace, as well as to deliver mail and supplies to farms along the way.

You can see remnants of a steamboat at Bay City Lodge

The picturesque setting along the Apalachicola River became the scene of a terrible slaughter in 1816.

north of where Apalachicola is today and fifty miles south of the then-border of the United States. Six years later, when Andrew Jackson and American troops drove the British out of Pensacola, the British, under the leadership of Colonel Edward Nicholls, established an earthen fort five hundred feet from the river at Prospect Bluff. The British then recruited runaway slaves from the Carolinas and Georgia and some Native Americans to hold the fort and control traffic on the river. After Colonel Nicholls built the fort there, he wanted Indian trader Hawkins to look into the injustices supposedly caused by the Americans and thus put a wedge between the Indians and the Americans, dividing the two forces and maybe leading to a renewal of British influence in West Florida. Hawkins responded with the quotation above, probably referring to a treaty that the British had with the Native Americans.

In April, 1815, the British left the fort, but supplied its inhabitants with guns and ammunition. African Americans, who later established farms along the river and raised corn to support their families, would flee to the fort when danger approached. The Native Americans in the vicinity did not use the fort very much because they were less skilled at fighting from confined spaces than at guerrilla-type tactics that relied on ambushes and stealth.

The fort became known as the "Negro Fort." Its inhabitants continued to control traffic on the river from the fort's vantage point fifteen feet above the water. At a time when the area had few good roads, the river acted as a natural highway into southern Alabama and Georgia. Because a swamp at the back of the fort protected it from a land attack, the fort's inhabitants knew an attack would have to come from the river. When the African Americans interfered with the passage of supply ships up the river in 1815–1816, federal troops moved into action.

General Andrew Jackson, after his victory over the British at New Orleans in January, 1815, demanded that the Spanish, who still controlled west Florida, abolish the Negro Fort and disburse those manning it. When he received no reply from the Spanish, he ordered his troops to destroy the fort and take control of the area. As Native American resi-

dents of villages along the river heard of the approaching soldiers, they took refuge in the fort. On July 27, 1816, a federal boat sailed up the river before anchoring three thousand
yards below the fort near the western shore of the river at a
place called Forbes Island. At the same time, Lieutenant
Colonel Duncan Clinch led a group of 116 soldiers and 150
Creek allies down the river from Fort Scott, which was on the
Flint River a few miles north of the Florida line, and met the
gunboat sent up from Apalachicola.

When the fort's defenders spotted the boats the next
morning, they fired at them, but could not hit them. The federal gunboats fired light cannon shot at the fort, basically to
gauge the distance, and then someone on the boat decided to
heat a cannon ball before lobbing it into the fort. The hot pro-
jectile breached the wall of the fort, entered the powder magazine, and caused an immense explosion that killed over two
hundred of the three hundred people in the fort—men,
women, and children. The survivors abandoned the fort and
fled into the forest.

Two years later, at the start of the First Seminole War,
General Jackson returned to the area with a force of soldiers,
determined to rid the place of the Native Americans once and
for all. Because of the strategic location of the fort, he had one
of his engineers, Lieutenant James Gadsden of the Engineer
Corps, rebuild it as a supply depot, which was later renamed
Fort Gadsden. Lieutenant Gadsden was also responsible for
the Gadsden Purchase, by which the U.S. bought thirty thousand square miles from Mexico in 1853; this land now forms
part of Arizona and New Mexico. Gadsden County, which is
north of Franklin County and borders Alabama, also honors
that officer.

It took only ten days to restore the fort. Jackson went on
to destroy Indian villages; capture the Spanish fort at St.
Marks, south of Tallahassee; arrest and execute two British
traders (Arbuthnot and Ambrister), whom he accused of
inciting the Native Americans to revolt; advance on
Pensacola, which was then a Spanish stronghold; successfully
demand that the Spanish surrender their forts; and set up an
American military government in West Florida—all of which

led to the Spanish ceding Florida to the United States in 1821. American troops occupied Fort Gadsden until 1821, but—after the threat from Native Americans and runaway slaves had diminished—abandoned it.

In 1818, while Jackson's army was still at Fort Gadsden, one of the soldiers stationed there, Duncan McKrimmon, went fishing, but lost his way and was captured by Native Americans. They were from a nearby place on the Wakulla River called Francis's Town, which was named after Francis the Prophet, a Creek chief whose Creek Indian name was Hillis Hadjo and who allied his followers with the British. The younger of Francis's two daughters, a teenager named Malee (later anglicized to "Milly"), who was present at the time McKrimmon was going to be executed, convinced his captors from the tribe to spare McKrimmon. They later released him to the Spanish at Fort St. Marks, who let him go. Soon after that, U.S. forces captured Francis the Prophet and hanged him.

A few months later, Francis's family and other Native Americans surrendered and were taken to Fort Gadsden. Duncan McKrimmon went to Fort Gadsden and offered to marry Milly, but she refused. She was sent west to Indian Territory (present-day Oklahoma), where she married and had several children. In 1842, a Lieutenant Colonel Hitchcock searched for her and found her in Indian Territory, where she was raising her three young children. By this time, she was widowed and very poor. He initiated action which led to a Congressional act giving her a pension of $96 a year and a medal for her part in the release of Duncan McKrimmon. A plaque at Fort Gadsden recounts these events.

During the Civil War, Confederate officials strongly considered obstructing the river near Fort Gadsden in order to keep Union vessels from sailing up the Apalachicola to the boat-construction facilities at Columbus, Georgia. The depth and width of the river near the fort made an obstruction very feasible. The elevation of the fort above the river gave it a commanding position, good roads offered access to the sea, and the swamp on both sides of the river hindered any land attack on the fort. Because the Apalachicola widened considerably below that point, the fort was actually the most southerly point on the river for such an obstruction. The main problem was the unhealthy location for quartering troops, which the Confederate officers realized in 1863, when an onset of malaria forced their troops to withdraw. The officers, in the end, chose other places farther up the river for the obstruction, and the abandoned fort remained uninhabited for over a hundred years.

In 1961, the Florida Park Service leased seventy-eight acres of land from local owners to operate a facility there. When archaeologists began examining the site, they found artifacts such as musket balls, nails, fish hooks, beer bottles, and knives, as well as a cemetery—all remnants of the fort's long history.

Today, the place is called Fort Gadsden State Historic Site and features displays, artifacts, and explanations of the fort and its importance in the history of Florida. Also on the property are remnants of an old steamer, the *Irvington*, that sank in the Apalachicola River in 1838 and was retrieved for display. The steamer was carrying two hundred bales of cotton when it burned and sank on a down-river run four miles upstream.

Visitors can reach Fort Gadsden by driving along SR 65 on the eastern side of the Apalachicola River. The site is six miles south of Sumatra and twenty miles north of Highway 98. Look carefully for the small sign indicating the turn-off to Fort Gadsden, which is about three miles from SR 65. The three-mile stretch of road connecting SR 65 with Fort Gadsden State Park was named the Eddie J. NeSmith Road by the Franklin County Commission in 2002, in honor of the ranger who compiled the area's historical record.

Fort Gadsden State Historic Site is listed in the National Register of Historic Places. Visitors who may marvel at the peace and serenity of the idyllic spot overlooking the river may have a hard time imagining the terrible tragedy that occurred there in 1816. Visitors must pay a small fee and may not use mineral or metal detectors, magnetometers, sidescan sonars, or other metal-detecting devices. See Visitor Information for more.

14.

LANARK AND ST. JAMES
ISLAND

"Life at Lanark Village is beautiful and satisfying and

you can live for less. You can own your own comfortable

low-cost home and hardly touch a penny of your savings.

Small down payment and as little as $39.50 per month

will cover interest and pay off your mortgage."

—1950s Lanark Estates advertisement

T HE SMALL RETIREMENT COMMUNITY six miles east of
Carrabelle has a quiet about it that belies its World War
II history. Its name, which is pronounced LAN-ark, comes
from Scottish *lan* (land) and *ark* (place of refuge). The presi-
dent of the Organization of the Scottish Land and
Improvement Company, a New Jersey–based company which
bought and sold land in the 1890s in Florida, was from
Lanarkshire, Scotland.

The village, which in the past was called Lanark-on-the-
Gulf and Lanark Springs, was begun in the nineteenth century by the Georgia, Florida, and Alabama Railroad as a fashionable resort for Floridians. Officials, who chose the site of
the village along their railroad because of its accessibility and
proximity to the Gulf, built a two-story hotel with a large

Thousands of soldiers trained at Camp Gordon Johnston near Lanark during World War II.

veranda near the water. Guests could swim in the nearby Gulf in an area surrounded by a wire fence that kept out sharks and other predators. A natural spring twenty feet from the hotel could furnish fresh water for up to five thousand people a day and provided a place where those who believed in the healing powers of such waters could immerse themselves. Soon the clientele came to include Georgians who wanted a vacation spot on the Gulf of Mexico.

When World War II began, the federal government realized that new tactics and operations were needed to fight a war on several fronts and engage the enemy in a new type of battle. For example, instead of a costly overland attack on the enemy, especially in the Pacific theater, where jungle terrain and impenetrable land defenses made a frontal attack very risky, officers in the U.S. Army and Navy realized that a ship-to-shore attack by water-borne troops would be much more effective as they outflanked the enemy.

The first place chosen for training Allied troops in this new type of warfare was Camp Edwards, Massachusetts, mostly because of the urgent need to use existing housing, supply, and communication facilities near a body of water (Vineyard Sound) that provided different kinds of beaches and islands. Headquarters of the Engineer Amphibian Command were set up there in June, 1942.

When winter weather impeded, then stopped, training at the Massachusetts site, the War Department searched for a sparsely settled place near the sea with suitable beaches and sufficient ground area for a new base. The area around Lanark was chosen as the best site. Work began in the middle of 1942 with the surveying of 165,000 acres leased from the St. Joe Paper Company and the preparation of twenty-one miles of coastal land along the Gulf of Mexico for what would be known as Camp Gordon Johnston. In October, 1942, the Second Engineer Special Brigade and the Army Ground Forces Amphibious Training Center moved in to complete their training. When the Second Brigade shipped out to fight in the Pacific, the Third Brigade moved in to train with the Thirty-eighth Division.

Around a quarter of a million soldiers trained at Camp

Gordon Johnston, the second largest military facility in the state at the time. The name of the camp honored a colonel who had served in the cavalry in the early twentieth century, won a Medal of Honor for his actions in the Philippines, and later fought in France during World War I.

The presence of thousands of soldiers in Carrabelle—which had only about one thousand residents in 1940—had an enormous effect. It strained local facilities, for example, in terms of housing for soldiers' wives with local families because of a lack of base housing. Some other problems were procuring enough landing craft and other equipment, finding enough warm clothes for some particularly cold Florida winters, and providing adequate transportation to take the soldiers to outside towns. Nonetheless, the local people did their best to welcome the soldiers. County Judge R.M. Witherspoon, for example, ruled that all servicemen could hunt and fish in Franklin County without licenses, a small token of appreciation for the many servicemen who trained there.

The camp's soldiers specialized in amphibious landings, a skill they used when they fought in the Pacific and European theaters. General Omar Bradley, who would become the leader of the American Ground Forces in France during World War II, trained in Camp Gordon Johnston. In 1944, the Allies sent German and Italian prisoners to the camp. In April, 1946, one year after the end of the war, the camp was closed, and all the lands of the camp were transferred, sold, or returned to the former owners, in particular St. Joe Paper Company, which received thirty-seven thousand dollars to restore the area to what it had been before the war. In 1957, the Air Force bought a small portion of the camp's land in Carrabelle for a tracking station in support of Tyndall Air Force Base in Panama City to the west.

Once the war ended and Camp Johnston closed, the area lost hundreds of soldiers, but life returned to the pre-war business of making a living and raising families. No longer dependent on income generated by the military, residents of Franklin County returned to what they had done before: oystering, fishing, timbering, and selling goods. The development that changed the landscape of South Florida so dramatically around this time bypassed Franklin County and solidified its reputation as the "Forgotten Coast."

No one knows how many of the soldiers stationed at Camp Gordon Johnston returned to Apalachicola Bay after the war to visit or live, but the number is probably quite high. It would take several decades after the end of the war before the county began to thrive once again, but when outsiders discovered the area's beautiful climate and living conditions, they would often come to visit or live.

In 1954, a Miami-based corporation, Lanark Estates, Inc., bought much of the land and buildings that had comprised Camp Gordon Johnston, opened up offices in New York, Chicago, and Washington, and began promoting the village as a beautiful and affordable place to live. Property prices ranged from less than five thousand dollars for an efficiency to less than eight thousand for a three-bedroom apartment.

The Lanark Village Association was formed in 1956 to act as a liaison between management and residents and to help residents get to know each other. Among the improvements in the next four decades were an American Legion Post (1957), the acquisition of a second-hand bus for trips to nearby sites (1959), the establishment of a Boat Club (1960) and Golf Club (1961), the formation of the St. James–Lanark Volunteer Fire Department (1975), and the building of the first firehouse (1990), all of which made the retirement village a more appealing place to live.

East and northeast of Lanark Village, towards Ochlockonee Bay, are several settlements, including Turkey Point, Wilson Beach, St. Teresa Beach, and St. James Island. St. Teresa Beach, named for a woman named Teresa Hopkins (the addition of "St." to the name remains a mystery), was settled in the mid-1870s by people from Tallahassee who wanted to live closer to their favorite vacation spots than in Virginia and North Carolina.

Still farther east are Southern Dunes, Lighthouse Point, Alligator Point, Peninsula Point, and Alligator Beach. St. James Island, a very large, mostly undeveloped area formed by the confluence of the Crooked and Ochlockonee Rivers to the north and the Gulf of Mexico to the south, has many natural resources and the potential to become the site of a large marina and large-scale development by St. Joe Land Development Corporation. In order to ensure protection of the area's natural resources, the Apalachee Ecological Conservancy, Inc. (APECO) has developed a plan and campaign to push for balanced growth and development in the area.

Alligator Point was the home of novelist Connie May Fowler in the early 1990s. Her published novels include *Sugar Cage* (1992), *River of Hidden Dreams* (1994), *Before Women Had Wings* (1996), and *Remembering Blue* (2000). The last one is set on Dog Island (renamed Lethe in the novel) and Carrabelle.

Scientists and environmentalists have long realized the importance of the area and have taken steps to preserve it for future generations. Florida State University established its Marine Edward Ball Laboratory at Turkey Point in 1968 to study the Gulf and nearby waters. The facility is particularly well situated for the study of marine biology and oceanography because the water there is virtually free of pollution and can be pumped into tanks to reproduce the exact temperature and conditions of the Gulf of Mexico at different locations. Named in honor of benefactor Edward Ball, the complex has over a dozen laboratories, a classroom, a house, and a dozen boats. In the labs, virtually every marine organism native to the Florida Panhandle has been examined by biologists, professors, and graduate students from around the country who live and do research on the premises. Scientists have experimented with the cross-breeding of Central American oysters in order to produce a hybrid oyster that would be immune to parasites and parasitic worms (called drills) and large enough to be commercially viable. Other projects involve mollusks, scallops, and varied marine life, and promise to have far-reaching effects in fields such as medicine and ecology. Much of the research done at Turkey Point has led to better use of Apalachicola Bay and promoted its long-term survival.

Officials designated over fourteen thousand acres of submerged tidal wetlands as the Alligator Harbor Aquatic Preserve in 1969 and established Bald Point State Park between Ochlockonee Bay and Alligator Harbor in 1999. The waters there provide good saltwater fishing and other recreational opportunities, and the bays provide foraging habitat for rare birds and sea turtles, including juvenile Kemp's ridley sea turtles, the world's most endangered sea turtle.

Today, Lanark Village is a quiet retirement community near the Gulf with about a thousand residents, many of whom are original settlers (or descendants) who migrated from the Northeast and Midwest after seeing newspaper ads in the 1950s that described the wonderful setting of the town. It has a par-three golf course, a yacht club, boat ramps, waterfront camping, motels, a fire department, and a post office. Where the major highway (US 98/SR 30) crosses Ochlockonee Bay northeast of Lanark Village, drivers have their last view of the Gulf from a main highway until the Tampa Bay area, some 250 miles down the coast. The land between the Gulf and the main highways in that stretch is swampy and inaccessible by ordinary vehicle.

As with other small communities, Lanark relies on a volunteer fire department to handle the emergencies that occur every year. The St. James Lanark Volunteer Fire Department, with help from fire trucks provided by the Forestry Department or bought from other towns with contributions, has answered hundreds of calls and prevented widespread damage.

Plans for development of the area include the creation by Arvida (which is part of St. Joe Company) of SummerCamp, a beach-front vacation community on 766 acres near the intersection of Highways 98 and 319.

15.

CARRABELLE

The heat in the summer is one hundred and ten

Too hot for the Devil, too hot for the men.

Come see for yourself and you can tell

It's a helluva place, this Carrabelle.

—From a poem by a soldier training at Camp

Gordon Johnston during World War II

TWO YEARS AFTER THE UNITED STATES TOOK control of the Florida territory from Spain in 1821, two men set out, one from St. Augustine in the east and one from Pensacola in the west, to find a midway point where the new territorial capital could be established. The man from Pensacola, attorney John Williams, encountered a hurricane near Apalachicola Bay and took shelter with his party at the mouth of Crooked River, near present-day Carrabelle. Eventually, he and the man from St. Augustine established the new capital at Tallahassee, the midpoint between the two cities. If the men had met at Carrabelle and established that site as the capital, how different the history of Franklin County would have been.

The town of Carrabelle, which has been called the Pearl of the Panhandle, is actually on an island, bounded by the Carrabelle, Crooked, and Ochlockonee Rivers. It has a population of 1,303, according to the 2000 census, which represents an increase of 103 (or about ten people per year) since

The deep channel near Carrabelle has allowed boats of all sizes to use its facilities.

1990. The town has 562 households, the median age is 40.8, and 91.5% of the people are white.

Carrabelle is also the name of the nearby river, which enters St. George Sound twenty-two miles east of Apalachicola after two other rivers, the New and Crooked Rivers, have joined to form it. Where the Carrabelle enters St. George Sound, there is excellent saltwater and freshwater fishing.

The origin of the name of the town/river is debatable. One theory says that it comes from the founder of the place, Oliver Hudson Kelley, a man from Massachusetts who helped found the National Grange, a farmers' organization that enabled farmers in the Midwest to unite for better conditions. Kelley, convinced that the Florida site would prosper with the lumber and seafood industries, bought almost two thousand acres of land near the water in 1877, moved there with his wife and children, and built a hotel, Island House, that his niece, Carolyn Arrabell Hall, managed. Kelley named the community Rio Carrabelle after his niece. The name was later shortened to Carrabelle. Another theory about the name states that a Spanish explorer, Pánfilo de Narváez, named the town *Rio Carrabella,* or "Beautiful River." Either way, the name was changed to Carrabelle three years after the federal government established the town's first post office in 1878.

The town developed in the late nineteenth century because of the timber and naval stores industries. With backing from Northern investors, Kelley had a railroad built from Carrabelle to Tallahassee in 1893. The rail and sea connections helped Carrabelle thrive. The town was incorporated in 1893, and over nine hundred people had settled in by 1900. As the timber industry brought some prosperity to the area, more people moved in, stores were built, and a newspaper operated.

Carrabelle and Apalachicola competed for the lumber and seafood industries as well as for representation before the state of Florida. They did manage to compromise in the field of politics by alternating the two-year seat in the Florida House of Representatives that the district was entitled to.

Like Apalachicola and Eastpoint, Carrabelle takes much

of its identity from the sea. Its waterfront, which today has a Coast Guard Station and the Florida Marine Patrol Headquarters, has been favorably compared to waterfront towns in New England and the West Coast. You can see a wide range of boats, from the small, privately owned to the large, eighty-foot-long shrimp boats. Private parties of fishermen can launch their boats from one of several launch spots in town.

But unlike other towns along the Gulf coast, Carrabelle has not depended totally on a harvest from the sea. Instead it has relied on the timber and turpentine industries, and, during the Civil War, on salt production. Its favorable location enabled the Air Force to set up a Ranging Station in the 1970s; this facility uses five tall towers in the Gulf of Mexico to track aircraft in the area.

Its location at the northern edge of the Gulf of Mexico exposed Carrabelle to the danger of hurricanes. An 1899 hurricane destroyed most of the homes in Carrabelle and killed several people. The docks along the waterfront were all destroyed, along with several hundred thousand feet of lumber and fifty thousand barrels of rosin that were waiting to be shipped elsewhere. Forty sailing vessels and cargo ships were wrecked; remnants from those ships kept washing ashore for years afterwards.

Like much of the country, Carrabelle suffered during the Great Depression, but tried new industries to survive, for example, a mattress factory that the Federal Emergency Relief Administration (FERA) helped fund. In 1947, the town lost its railroad connection to the north, probably because of the lack of passengers and freight, but the building of good roads since then has compensated for the loss of the railroad.

One advantage that Carrabelle had over its western rival was a deep channel that could be dredged to twenty-five feet. In World War II, that deep-water facility enabled lumber companies in Franklin County to ship thousands of pine and cypress poles for use in the construction of barbed-wire obstructions at the Maginot Line in France. Around that same time, the threat of German U-boats off the coast of Florida, including the Gulf of Mexico, necessitated the building of an oil pipeline overland to Jacksonville from near Carrabelle, which was at the eastern end of the barge zone of the Gulf Intracoastal Waterway. The oil would come by barge, was offloaded into the pipeline, and was shipped overland to avoid the dangers of shipping it by open water around Florida. After the war, the pipeline was dismantled and its operation discontinued. One remnant of World War II that is still standing in Carrabelle is the town's airport, Thompson Field.

The strategic location of Carrabelle at the eastern end of the protected Intracoastal Waterway allowed it to attract barges transporting wheat flour in bulk from the Midwest via the Missouri-Mississippi river system. In Carrabelle, workers removed the flour to bulk storage and then transported it to large trucks, which then transported it to major commercial bakeries.

The Intracoastal Waterway attracts many boaters along the northern Gulf of Mexico. In the past, boaters used to rely on the Crooked River Lighthouse to navigate the offshore waters. In 1995, officials decommissioned the lighthouse, but six years later deeded the lighthouse to Carrabelle. The Carrabelle Lighthouse Association has plans to restore the structure and open it to the public along with a museum highlighting the area's maritime history. (For more about the lighthouse, see the next chapter.)

More recently the town has become famous for having what it claims is the "World's Smallest Police Station," which consists of a telephone booth. Back in 1963, the station's phone used to be located in a call box bolted to the building at the corner of Tallahassee Street and US 98. People used to make unauthorized long-distance phone calls on the police phone, and the policemen used to get drenched when they answered the phone during a rainstorm. When the telephone company decided to replace an old phone booth in front of Burda's Pharmacy with a new one, it put the police phone in the old booth and moved it to a drier place under a large tree on US 98. The World's Smallest Police Station was thus "opened." A Carrabelle policeman can often be found near the phone booth, waiting for a distress call, watching for speeding motorists, and answering the many queries from interested tourists. The station has been featured on television shows such as *Real People* and *The Today Show* as well as in print media in English and other languages. The television shows alone have reached more than seven million people—all potential tourists who may have never heard of the town otherwise, but who saw Carrabelle as a peaceful, clean city with a picturesque harbor and a real charm about it.

Of related interest is the fact that Lloyd W. Smith, a 1956 graduate of Carrabelle High School, was named commander of the Metropolitan Police Department's Second District in the nation's capital in 1979. His policemen were in charge of handling any trouble near the White House or nearby foreign embassies. Other locals who went on to distinguished careers include Richard Ervin, who was born in Carrabelle in 1905 and later went on to become attorney general and chief justice of the Florida Supreme Court. A stone plaque honoring him is at Veterans' Park along US 98, near the center of town. That park also has a Freedom Fountain that honors Carrabelle's military veterans. Dr. E. Roy Solomon, a Carrabelle native, became the dean of the College of Business at Florida State University (FSU) and the recipient of the Midyette Chair of Insurance at FSU. James B. Powers of Burda Pharmacy was named Pharmacist of the Year in 1990 by the American Pharmaceutical Association. Mack Mangham's novel, *The Accidental Agent,* takes place in the area. The town is also the site of the movie *Coastlines,* during the filming of which the C-Quarters Restaurant was transformed into the Blue Crab Lounge.

Of even more fame is the way the residents of Carrabelle began celebrating Independence Day in the early part of the twentieth century. The Franklin Firecracker Festival had a parade, lots of food, music, crafts, dancing, and—of course—fireworks. The local railroad would bring in an excursion train full of people from as far away as Cuthbert, Georgia, many of whom would spend a dollar for the customary round-trip boat ride to Dog Island. Once on the island, people could use the public pavilion and dressing rooms that the city of Carrabelle had set up. Many local people would join them for a day of swimming, fishing, and picnicking before returning to Carrabelle. The lumber mills and ice plant would blow their steam whistles that day—but what made Carrabelle's celebration truly different was the practice of pouring a barrel of gasoline on the river and then lighting it, making a spectacular scene, especially at night. (That practice has been discontinued.)

The Chamber of Commerce holds the annual Carrabelle Waterfront Festival in April, which features a gumbo cook-off. The 1997 winner, Jackie Gay, went on to win the *Good Housekeeping Magazine* Recipe of the Year contest as well as fifty thousand dollars from actor Paul Newman's Foundation. She donated the sum to the Franklin County Public Library System, and the State of Florida matched it, enabling Carrabelle to have a new library in 2002. A local newspaper dubbed the Carrabelle branch of the county library "the library that gumbo built."

Other popular events include the annual Father's Day Weekend Big Bend Saltwater Fishing Classic and the annual Boat Parade of Lights on the Carrabelle River. Fishing is so good around Carrabelle that the Florida Fish and Wildlife Conservation Commission holds a Kids Fishing Clinic, a one-day event to instruct youngsters about responsible angling, conservation, and habitat protection, as well as to help them catch fish.

Carrabelle never became the capital of Florida and not even of Franklin County, but it has managed to survive economically and, in a sense, reinvent itself to attract more residents and more business while maintaining a small-town atmosphere that bodes well for the future.

16.

CARRABELLE BEACH
AND SURROUNDINGS

"O listen, good people, a story I'll tell of a great swamp in

Florida, a place called Tate's Hell; a hundred and forty

watery miles with millions of skeeters and big yellow flies."

—Will McLean, "Tate's Hell" (a ballad)

Will McLean, Florida's famed "Black-hat Troubadour," sang about a hunter from Sumatra named Tate who, while hunting a panther in the forbidding swamp northwest of Carrabelle Beach in the late 1800s, was bitten by a rattlesnake and died a painful death as he staggered near Carrabelle. Though it is relatively uninhabited, there is nothing eerie about Carrabelle Beach or the surrounding area. With a combination of a pretty beach on the Gulf, a lighthouse that can be viewed up close, a historic site (Camp Gordon Johnston's training area), and a rich forest in its proximity, Carrabelle Beach appeals to many different kinds of people.

Carrabelle Beach's Wayside Park off the coastal highway has free parking, picnic tables, and public restrooms for beachgoers. Completed in 1971, it had its flagpole dedication in 2002. Beach bathers and picnickers today may have a hard

The Crooked River Lighthouse near Carrabelle Beach marks the eastern end of the western section of Florida's Intracoastal Waterway.

time imagining Carrabelle Beach being overrun by hundreds of soldiers in amphibious vehicles attacking a fictitious enemy that lurked just inshore, but that is what happened during World War II. Soldiers used the beaches all along Franklin County, especially from Carrabelle Beach up toward Lanark Village, to prepare for the D-Day Invasion and other military actions toward the end of the war. A plaque at Carrabelle Beach honoring those soldiers reads as follows:

> **World War II D-Day Training Site.** In late 1943 Carrabelle Beach and Dog Island, while they were a part of Camp Gordon Johnston, were used by the U.S. Army 4th Infantry Division to train for the Normandy Invasion on D-Day, June 6th, 1944. The Amphibious Training Center had been officially closed, but it was reopened and staffed for the purpose of training for this important mission. Although the troops had trained for over three years, the amphibious training conducted on this site was the last step before shipping out to England for the invasion. On D-Day, the first amphibian infantry assault teams to arrive on French soil were from the 4th Infantry Division at Utah Beach. On June 6, 2000, the Camp Gordon Johnston Association extracted a small amount of soil from this site and delivered it to the National 4th Infantry Division Association to be placed in the Association's monument in Arlington, VA. The U.S. Department of Defense's World War II Commemoration Committee in 1995 named the Camp Gordon Johnston Association an official "Commemorative Community."

This plaque is just one of many that honor the 248,000 Floridians who served in the military during World War II and the six hundred thousand veterans from that war who made their home in Florida.

The Crooked River Lighthouse, also known as the Carrabelle Lighthouse, is located about 2.1 miles west of the Tillie Miller Bridge leading to Carrabelle. The skeletal iron structure was built in 1893 and lit in 1895 to replace a lighthouse that a hurricane had destroyed on Dog Island in 1873.

The lower half of the tower is white, its upper half, dark red. The structure was designed to be dismantled if necessary. The tower had a fourth-order Fresnel lens 115 feet above the sea. The original lens for the lighthouse, which still exists today, may have been the first bivalve-style lens ever installed in a lighthouse in this country. During the lighthouse's heyday, only two keepers operated it instead of the usual three—an indication that federal authorities did not consider this tower to be of the utmost importance. When one of the two keepers had to be away on business, the other had to take over all of the duties. When the area's timber business declined in the first half of the twentieth century and Carrabelle lost in importance to Apalachicola, the town and its lighthouse remained relatively untouched by the outside world.

The lighthouse was revived briefly during World War II as it guided oil tankers coming into Carrabelle to fill a pipeline that carried petroleum to Jacksonville. In the mid-1960s, the Coast Guard auctioned both lighthouse keepers' houses, which were then moved 2.2 miles west. Fire destroyed one of the houses; the other is now a private residence. In 2001, the tower was turned over to the City of Carrabelle to be managed and restored by a non-profit volunteer organization called the Carrabelle Lighthouse Association. The lighthouse marks the eastern end of the western section of Florida's Intracoastal Waterway and is listed on the National Register of Historic Places.

Near the beach is Timber Island, a picturesque island where wild goats used to roam. Leading from the island to Carrabelle is the Tillie Miller Bridge, named after the late, long-time resident who came to the area with her husband in 1924 and who was a friend, advisor, midwife, and sometimes doctor to the people of Carrabelle for forty-three years. The bridge, which was completed in 1977, replaced one that had been built in 1928.

The many "For Sale" signs on the land along Highway 98 between Eastpoint and Carrabelle Beach indicate that development is slowly coming in. The road there is so close to the water that hurricanes have washed over it and stopped traffic for many hours. Hurricanes Elena, Juan, and Kate in the fall of

1985 washed away sections of the road and made travel very difficult, but today people continue to buy land near the water and build houses that can withstand minor hurricanes.

Midway between Eastpoint and Carrabelle Beach is a section called Royal Bluff. The dunes along the water, especially the ancient and locally well-known "Yellow Hill," show geologists how the sea level has fluctuated over thousands of years. The levels changed greatly from the Miocene Epoch (about twenty-five million years ago), when the sea level was three hundred feet above present levels, to the Pliocene Epoch (about fifteen million years ago), when the sea level was one hundred feet below present levels. The fluctuation that formed the Royal Bluff dunes is probably still going on, with the possible result that, as the sea level rises over the next thousand years, much of Florida will be inundated.

Tate's Hell State Forest is located between the Apalachicola and Ochlockonee rivers and borders the southwest boundary of Apalachicola National Forest. Tate's Hell State Forest covers 144,508 acres, mostly in Franklin County with a small part in the southern part of Liberty County. The Buckeye Cellulose Corporation, which owns a great deal of land around the Tate's Hell Swamp and maintains the Gully Branch Area for public use, has built seven hundred miles of roads in Tate's Hell and encourages hunters, fishermen, and boaters to use the forest, but many are reluctant to enter because of the dense underbrush and the fables associated with it. A short movie produced by the College of Communication at Florida State University around 1983, "A Tale From Tate's Hell," depicts the legendary Cebe Tate, after whom the swamp is named. The film tells about the efforts of a fictional anthropologist and her husband to free Tate from an ancient Creek curse that condemned him to roam the swamp forever.

Because of its mostly wet habitat, thick underbrush, and hordes of insects, Tate's Hell is largely uninhabited by humans, although many other creatures live there. The forest harbors dwarf cypresses, which are, in some cases, over one hundred and fifty years old—but only fifteen feet tall. Some can be seen from the boardwalk named in honor of the late

Ralph G. Kendrick, who was Franklin County Commissioner from 1980 to 1984, an avid hunter and outdoorsman, an employee at the Florida Division of Forestry, and an advocate for the preservation of the dwarf cypresses. The animals in the swamp include the eastern diamondback rattlesnake, eastern box turtle, gopher tortoise, bald eagle, barred owl, red-cockaded woodpecker, red-shouldered hawk, wild turkey, deer, and black bear.

In the early 1950s, timber companies tried to drain the swamp in order to harvest trees, but that changed when environmentalists pointed out that draining the swamp's fresh water into the East Bay and depleting its vegetation would hurt Apalachicola Bay's water quality. In 1994, officials with the Conservation and Recreation Lands Program (CARL) began buying lands in the forest in order to preserve the estuarine resources of the bay for posterity.

The purchase of 3,406 acres in Tate's Hell State Forest by the Nature Conservancy from the St. Joe Company in 2001 helped the Florida Chapter of the Nature Conservancy reach a milestone: the protection of its millionth acre of natural Florida. Only two other Nature Conservancy chapters in the country have accomplished that feat. Various organizations protect about twenty-three percent of the state's thirty-five million acres and are aiming to conserve a total of one-third of the state. The Franklin County purchase, which protects cypress swamps, flatwoods, rivers, streams, and wet prairies, will provide critical protected habitat for Florida black bears and help keep as pure as possible the water that flows into Apalachicola Bay and nearby estuaries.

17.

EASTPOINT

"[In 1935] the John Gorrie Bridge was opened and linked Apalachicola with Eastpoint and places beyond. It was six and a half miles of concrete ribbon that stood for hope and people by the thousands celebrated its grand opening."
—William W. Rogers and Lee Willis, III, *At the Water's Edge*

EASTPOINT IS THE TOWN IMMEDIATELY to the east of Apalachicola across the bay. It was named for its geographical position on the east point of a peninsula and to the east of Apalachicola (which used to be known as West Point). The town name used to be two words, but was contracted in order to distinguish it from East Point, Georgia. Eastpoint residents have occasionally suggested that the town should have the Franklin County seat because of its central location between Apalachicola and Carrabelle. That has not come to pass, but Eastpoint has continued to grow slowly. The town and its environs have, according to the 2000 census, a population of 2,158 inhabitants, 96.6% of whom are white. The median age is 36.3.

The town has water on three sides: St. George Sound to the east, Apalachicola Bay to the south, and East Bay to the north. It also has tidal flats on the bay side of the barrier islands, in the shallow waters near marshes, and along the mainland. Marine biologists consider these flats very impor-

The fishing and oyster boats of Eastpoint have easy access to the rich waters of the bay.

tant to aquatic ecosystems because of their high microalgae production. A deep-water channel enables commercial fishermen to bring their boats close to the dock. The Eastpoint Breakwater protects the channel and the boats docking there. The Breakwater, built in 1984 at the urging of civic-minded people like Xuripha Miller, who spent years advocating it, enabled the fishing and oyster boats to use the docks there more easily.

Much of the land around East Bay has been bought through the programs known as Conservation and Recreation Lands (CARL) and Environmentally Endangered Lands (EEL). East Bay, bordered by vast marshes and swamps, is about three feet deep on average. The Apalachicola River empties into it, as do smaller waterways like the St. Marks, Little St. Marks, and East Rivers. One problem with East Bay is the occasional spread of Eurasian watermilfoil, an exotic aquatic plant that grows rapidly, forming a dense canopy on the water surface that inhibits water flow and is a navigational hazard and a threat to marine habitat. When it dies in the winter, it rots and sinks to the bottom, taking up oxygen and thus killing fish. Scientists are working to control or eliminate the weed.

The original settlers were Native Americans, although they probably lived much farther out into the Gulf of Mexico since the coastline of Florida used to be very different from what it is today. During the ice ages thousands of years ago, when large glaciers covered one fourth of the earth and contained much of the earth's water, the level of the oceans was as much as 350 feet lower than it is today. When Native Americans lived in Florida during the Paleoindian Period twelve thousand years ago, the size of Florida may have been twice its size today and the land stretched far out into the Gulf of Mexico. Because those sites are under the waters of the Gulf, archaeologists will probably not discover them for quite some time, if ever.

Indian Mound Acres, a historic site to the east of Eastpoint, commemorates in its name the fact that Native Americans used to live there before they were eliminated or relocated to the West by the federal government. The mounds they left behind were made from the discarding of thousands of shells from the shellfish they ate. They would throw the shells onto piles rather than littering their living space. Some of those mounds, called "middens" or "shell middens" or simply "shell mounds," are three or four stories high.

Nearby Cat Point, south of the bridge leading to Apalachicola, used to have several of those oyster mounds, but trucks hauled off the shells to use them in the paving of county roads in the first half of the twentieth century. This is why local residents sometimes find arrowheads, pot shards, and other artifacts along the roads. Because those mounds were often in prime locations, that is, in places with beautiful views of the Gulf, developers destroyed them to make room for the building of modern homes. Today, laws forbid the destruction of mounds on public lands.

White settlers established Eastpoint about 1896, when farmer David Brown and his family moved from the Midwest after helping to lead the People's or Populist Party, an organization dedicated to helping farmers. After leaving Nebraska, Brown and about seventy-five others settled in Columbus, Georgia, where they founded a collective farm to share the work and profits. Brown later convinced five families (the Allens, Browns, Griswells, McKeyes, and Thompsons) and two single men to head for Florida. They built two barges, which they sailed down the Chattahoochee and Apalachicola Rivers, bought land at Eastpoint, disassembled the barges to build their houses, and set up another collective farm called the Co-Workers' Fraternity, later changed to the Southern Co-Operative Association. The individuals owned their own land, but shared in the profits from lumbering, fishing, and commerce. Because the land was poor, the colony did not attract many others, and the town did not experience the growth its first planners had hoped for.

Cat Point used to have a ferry slip for the boat that carried people and freight to and from Apalachicola and St. George Island across the bay around 1900. An oyster-shucking plant, which employed only men, also stood there in the early part of the twentieth century. Several of the men, who had come from Baltimore, married local women and settled down in the area.

Eastpoint saw some action during the Civil War, although not as much as Apalachicola. For some time, two Union boats, the *Adela* and *Somerset,* were stationed near Eastpoint as part of the Union blockade to prevent shipping to and from Apalachicola Bay. A group of Confederates who had sailed down the Apalachicola River planned to attack the *Adela* and then escape up the river to safety, but their discovery by Union soldiers in Apalachicola and the scarcity of supplies forced them to abandon their attack plans and make a precarious escape back up the river.

In the late 1800s, Eastpoint grew steadily. The first official postmaster of the town was a Mr. Brown, but, because he was busy working his farm, the "unofficial" postmaster was his wife, Rebecca Brown, who signed her name "R.W. Brown" to hide her gender from the postal authorities. Beginning in 1898, she distributed the mail, which was brought to her home by boat. When she died in 1938, her husband took over as postmaster. Then their oldest son, Herbert "Egg" Brown, became postmaster. He had the benefit of a new postal facility in a new building in the center of town in the early 1940s. He served as postmaster until he retired at age seventy in 1953; the Eastpoint elementary school is named in his honor. His sister, Elizabeth Brown, took over for three years. One of her relatives, Donald Tucker, held the position from 1956 until 1960. Later, another Brown relative, Marjorie Hall, worked in the post office, finally retiring in 1986 after twenty-seven years in the job.

In 1935, workers employed by the federal government in efforts to stimulate the economy during the Great Depression built the John Gorrie Bridge, which links Eastpoint with Apalachicola. Until a new structure replaced it in 1988, operators manned the six-and-a-half mile, concrete swing-span bridge twenty-four hours a day, seven days a week to allow passage to boats with high masts.

While it retained its name, the structure was replaced in 1988 by a new thirteen-million-dollar concrete-and-steel bridge that rises sixty-five feet above the water . Workers dismantled the old bridge and towed it out to sea, where it became an artificial reef 10.7 nautical miles south-southeast of Bob Sikes Cut due south of St. George Island State Park. The material was enough to make two artificial reefs, each nine acres in size, taking up a total of seventy feet of federal waters. Both bridges brought in thousands of visitors to Franklin County, some of whom were so impressed by the beauty of the place that they settled down and raised families.

Another bridge from Eastpoint leads to St. George Island. It was finished in 1965 at a cost of four million dollars. The two-dollar toll to cross the bridge was ended in 1992, causing many on St. George Island to worry that the free bridge would attract many undesirables. A new four-mile-long bridge to St. George Island, which was finished in 2003, dips perilously close to the bay, which seems ready to wash over it in a hurricane. However, the connection of St. George Island to Eastpoint has no doubt given both towns more business than they might have had.

The town has a lively waterfront with seafood restaurants and oyster boats. The recent influx of new businesses such as furniture and home decorating businesses means that local home and beach cottage owners no longer have to go to Tallahassee or Panama City for certain kinds of goods. Among the best-known restaurants with a waterfront location is one with an unusual name: That Place on 98, which former golf pro Mike Keller runs. Among the local artists is Marcel Spencer, who, like her father, builds birdhouses that are studies in miniature of buildings around Franklin County. Former Eastpoint school teacher Lydia Countryman and Apalachicola Bay and River Keeper (ABARK), Inc., were honored in 2002 by the Council for Sustainable Florida for outstanding contributions to the state's long-term sustainability.

One of the field laboratories of the Florida Marine Research Institute is located at 350 Carroll Street in Eastpoint. With its headquarters in St. Petersburg, the institute employs over four hundred people statewide, most of whom are research and technical staff working to study and preserve Florida's maritime environment.

Between Eastpoint and Carrabelle to the east are mostly single-family homes owned by small landowners. As visitors drive along the coast of Apalachicola Bay, they may be surprised at the lack of development. In fact, the road to Carrabelle is surprisingly close to the bay, although the coastline has very little beach, the result of many years of the Gulf waters encroaching on the land and washing up against the pine stumps that used to stand on dry ground.

Part of the lack of development is due to the fact that state and federal governments own almost seventy percent of Franklin County and intend to keep most of it in its wild condition in order to provide future generations parks, unspoiled forests, and undeveloped land. Development is slowly coming into what has long been known as Florida's "Forgotten Coast," but regulations are meant to make such development conform to environmental laws. For example, the Franklin County Commission approved, in 2000, a 378-acre development called St. James Bay in the Apalachicola Flatwoods of the eastern part of the county, but that was the first large-scale development including a golf course that the commission has ever approved.

Because of its prime location at the mainland point of the bridge to St. George Island and the eastern point of the John Gorrie Memorial Bridge—plus the fact that fishing grounds lie on three sides of the town—Eastpoint has carved out an identity of its own. It may never be the county seat of Franklin County, as its residents once hoped, but its location has provided a good income and quality lifestyle for many people.

II.

APALACHICOLA

A PALACHICOLA, ACCORDING TO SOME AUTHORITIES, is a Hitchiti Indian word meaning "the people on the other side." Others say *apalachi* is a Choctaw word signifying "allies." As people began settling around the mouth of the Apalachicola River by the mid-1820s, the settlement became known as Cottonton because of the belief that cotton would determine its future economic growth. Then, in the late 1820s, it was known as West Point because of its geographical location on the river. Finally, in 1831, it became known as Apalachicola, to make the name conform to the name of the river and bay.

The Florida Legislature established Franklin County with Apalachicola as its county seat in 1832. Although the population figures for the county and city are incomplete for the early years of both, one scholar indicated that in 1828, four years before the county was established, it had only 100–150 people living in Apalachicola. The 1838 census indicated that Apalachicola had "1,890 whites, 169 slaves, and seven free

Negroes," for a total of 2,066.

In the 2000 census the town had a population of 2,334, while the county had a population of 11,057. In other words, more than one in five county residents live in Apalachicola. The town actually lost 268 residents or 10.3 percent from 1990. The slow rate of population growth for the town and county, while preventing them from generating much new income from taxes, has resulted in fewer pollutants being pumped into the bay, although environmentalists have had to be on the watch for pollutants from runoff from farms into the Apalachicola River and contamination of the river from Atlanta's aging water-pipe system.

The physical makeup of Apalachicola goes back to 1835, when the Apalachicola Land Company obtained clear title to the area by a U.S. Supreme Court decision. The following year, it began planning for a town whose carefully laid-out streets and parks would resemble the model city of the time, Philadelphia, Pennsylvania. Today the town has a two-and-a-half-square-mile historic district with more than two hundred historically and architecturally significant buildings.

Apalachicola is a good example of a town that has adapted to the times. It has had several rebirths: from a thriving cotton port before the Civil War to a major harvester of oysters in the twenty-first century; from a poor town along Florida's "Forgotten Coast" to a charming resort that has kept its old-fashioned aura; from a town on a bay famous for its private hunting preserve to an environmentally conscious community proud of its unique estuaries. How it reached this point involved both hard times and good, changes in direction, and some luck.

18.

DOWNTOWN APALACHICOLA

"Farewell, sandy, dry, hot Apalachicola.

May we never see thee more!"

—A Union soldier after the Civil War

HOW TIMES HAVE CHANGED! And how feelings toward the little town at the mouth of the Apalachicola River have fluctuated! The town's history is humble. It did not officially exist until President James Monroe appointed a port collector there in 1822, one year after the United States took control of Florida from Spain. But even after the establishment of an official port there, the prevalence of swamps and marshland, as well as the bay's relative shallowness, discouraged settlers from living there in great numbers for a long time.

Today, thousands of visitors come to Apalachicola each year. The John Gorrie Memorial Bridge gives first-time visitors coming from the east a spectacular view of Apalachicola: its watery boundaries (bay, river, wetlands), its historic downtown, the restored Gibson Inn hotel at the town's entrance, and the tall church steeples that dot the skyline.

The nearby waterfront is a good place for visitors to begin a tour of the town since a lot of its history and character

The Grady Building has served as a ship's chandlery, general store, and French consulate.

began there. Water Street used to be lined with buildings and warehouses as ships came up to the wharf for the loading and unloading of goods. Cotton bales filled the warehouses and piled up on the wharves 160 years ago, ready for shipment to Europe and the northeastern United States. The waterfront, which brought in ships and sailors and settlers, is where the town spread out from as it slowly expanded to the west.

The corner of Water and Chestnut Streets was the headquarters for the Apalachicola Land Company, which owned much of the land in the new settlement and which began selling lots, first to local residents, and then to outsiders, in 1836. The company was successful initially, selling over $400,000 worth of lots. But this changed as the Second Seminole War, a nationwide financial panic, and dissatisfaction with the Land Company made the new town less desirable. Such would be the history of the town; it would experience many fluctuations depending on outside factors and the changing tastes of visitors.

In 1838, on the east corner of Avenue E and Water Street, the Apalachicola Land Company built a cotton warehouse, which was one of over three dozen similar buildings along the river. Today's City Hall across the street was another cotton warehouse. The historical marker near the river on Avenue D and Water Street gives a brief summary of the town's history. Today, the working waterfront, which still has a few shrimp and oyster boats, also has motels and seafood restaurants.

Another remnant of the past, located between Water and Commerce Streets on Avenue E (Highway 98), is the *Venezelos,* an old shrimp boat that recalls the days when shrimping was an even more important part of the local economy. Built by a Greek-American, Demo George, it has a classic design and is a predecessor of the shrimp boats that still dock along Water Street.

The J.E. Grady Building at 76 Water Street, between Commerce and Water Streets, is a good example of how preservationists have been able to restore historically significant buildings. J.E. Grady (1853–1905) served as a representative in the Florida Legislature beginning in 1883 and as a senator in the same body beginning in 1893. He was also a customs collector for the port of Apalachicola and operated a ship chandlery located in a three-story cotton warehouse that was originally built in the 1840s and was rebuilt within a year after a 1900 fire that destroyed much of downtown. It served as a ship's chandlery and general store from 1884 until the mid-1920s. Its second floor housed a French consulate that was established in the early twentieth century to help French citizens who used the port for shipping out lumber and other goods. The location of the building in front of the docks made it convenient for ships' crews to buy supplies. It closed in the mid-1930s during the Great Depression, but has been carefully restored as the Grady Market with boutiques on the first floor that specialize in antiques, clothing, gourmet items, and unique gifts. The ex-consulate on the second floor now has four luxury suites for those who want to experience elegant living in the historic downtown.

The next street back from the water, Commerce Street, has the United States Post Office at Avenue D. Originally built as a customs house in 1923, the building today has a rare feature for a Florida building, a basement, as well as a tunnel that goes underground from the building to one across the street, its purpose unknown. The Sponge Exchange on the corner of Commerce Street and Avenue E dates back to 1840. It is one of two warehouses that stored sponges and represents the profitable sponging trade that took place in the bay in the nineteenth century.

The third street from the water, Market Street, has the Chamber of Commerce in the Apalachicola State Bank building at 99 Market Street. There, visitors can obtain brochures and maps, including details about a walking tour of the town. Near the chamber, at Market Street and Highway 98, the town's busiest corner, is the Apalachicola Seafood Grill & Steakhouse, which was featured in the opening scene of the movie *Ulee's Gold*. The restaurant, which is almost one hundred years old, claims to serve the world's largest fried-fish sandwich.

Apalachicola had one of Florida's first newspapers, *The Apalachicola Advertiser,* which was established in 1833, twelve years before Florida became a state. Today, the county's major newspapers are the *Apalachicola Times,* with offices at 82 Market Street, and *The Franklin Chronicle,* with offices in Eastpoint.

At 21 Avenue E between Commerce and Market streets is the Dixie Theatre, which dates back to 1912 and was the entertainment center of the county for several decades. Some of its predecessors include the New Pace Vaudeville Theatre (1909) and Dreamland (1910), the town's first movie theater, which had musicians to entertain patrons. The Dixie surpassed both of these with its curtained stage, sunken orchestra pit, balcony with private boxes, and colored lights outside that beckoned passers-by to enter. When tastes changed, the facility became a movie theater, but eventually closed in 1967. Today, the carefully restored building offers a professional drama repertory that runs from June through September.

At the corner of Market Street and Avenue F is one of the most beautiful homes in Apalachicola: the 1838 Raney House, which was built by David Greenway Raney and his wife, both from Virginia. The Greek Revival–style house was a center of political and social activities in its heyday. While three of the Raneys' sons served in the Confederacy, the rest of the family moved to Georgia for the duration of the war. During this time, Yankee forces in Apalachicola vandalized and probably would have burned the house down except that the wind was blowing in a direction opposite their plans. After the war, the Raneys returned to their adopted home, Apalachicola, where David Raney served two terms as mayor, promoted a short-lived race track, provided a theater for the cultural edification of his fellow townspeople, and prospered from the cotton business.

The two-story, four-column house has a portico, tall window shutters, and eight fireplaces. A large magnolia tree stands in the yard, which is surrounded by a white picket fence. The interior has chandeliers, an organ, and period pieces throughout. Over time, several owners have bought the house and lived in it. It went on the National Register of Historic Places in 1972. The City of Apalachicola bought it in 1973. It took ten years to restore it with money from local, state, and federal funds. In 2001, the Apalachicola Area

Historical Society began running it and overseeing extensive repairs to it. The house is open to the public.

Farther away from the downtown area, at 177 Fifth Street, is the 1838 Orman House, which Thomas Orman built in New York in 1838, shipped to Apalachicola, and installed over the harbor below. The property contains a barn, slave quarters, wells, and remnants of a facility that may have served as a convent, school, or infirmary during the Civil War. The main building has six fireplaces, wraparound porches, shuttered windows, period furniture, and a formal rose garden. In 1994, after forty-four years of neglect, the two-story house was restored by Annegret and Douglas Gaidry of Apalachicola. It stands today in its former grandeur. The State of Florida acquired the premises in 2000, and the Florida Department of Environmental Protection's Division of Recreation and Parks manages the house, which is open for tours and meetings. Near the house are the Chapman Botanical Gardens, which have a variety of flowers and commemorate one of the South's most famous botanists, Dr. Alvan Chapman (see chapter 23). See Visitor Information for details on all the sites mentioned in this chapter.

These are just a few landmark sites of a town that has slowly changed over the decades, and which, so far, has recognized how important its historic buildings are to preserving the past and to attracting visitors.

19.

INNS AND HOTELS

"Try to imagine what Florida's Gulf Coast must have looked like before timeshares, condo villages, and endless commercial and junk food strips appeared. Well, here at Apalachicola you'll discover all the charms of a so-called forgotten coast along with some splendid wildlife conservation areas. It's an irresistible, sweetly snoozing combination."

—Guide to Small Town Escapes

ONE OF THE BEST QUALITIES OF APALACHICOLA is the number of well-preserved or restored historic homes, many of which have become bed-and-breakfast establishments or places that visitors can tour at certain times. Because the Civil War did not damage many of those houses and because they were far enough away from the downtown area (which fires have sometimes ravaged), those homes look today like they did in the nineteenth century. In 1980, officials listed Apalachicola on the National Register of Historic Places because of its significant history and preservation projects. Avenue B is particularly noteworthy for its older homes.

Among the architectural features found on many of the older homes are long porches located downstairs and/or upstairs, often encircling the house, as well as towers and bay

The Coombs House Inn is an elegant Victorian mansion that offers the charm and historical authenticity of another era in a homelike atmosphere.

windows, especially for houses in the Queen Anne style. The town also has so-called "shotgun cottages," simply built houses for workers at the nearby lumber mills.

Five buildings in particular stand out, all large, elegant, and now in commercial use.

The Gibson Inn. The striking blue-and-white structure that visitors see in Apalachicola on crossing the John Gorrie Memorial Bridge is the Gibson Inn, (see photo on back cover). James Fulton "Jeff" Buck of South Carolina built it in 1907 as the Franklin Hotel, from hand-picked cypress on land he owned around East Bay. When the hotel opened in 1907, it charged $1.25 per night for a room. In the next decade and a half, the hotel went through some bad times as the tastes of tourists changed and visitors bypassed Apalachicola for more glamorous parts to the South.

In 1923, two sisters, Anne Gibson Hayes and Mary Ellen "Sunshine" Gibson, bought the Franklin and changed its name to Gibson Inn. The inn became a particular favorite of traveling salesmen, who would check in and then set up their displays of whatever they were selling (shoes, pots, clothes) for customers to stop by, see, and maybe order.

During World War II, the federal government took over the inn for use as an officers' club, but it soon returned to civilian use. For a nominal charge of four dollars a day, the hotel provided a room and three all-you-can-eat meals, a practice that threatened to bankrupt the facility when many hungry soldiers stopped by to take advantage of the great deal. That low price was soon stopped.

In 1983, after the inn had deteriorated badly, three out-of-towners bought the Victorian-style structure for around ninety thousand dollars and spent one million dollars over the next two years restoring it to its original beauty. One third of the cost of renovation came from the federal government's Community Block Grant Funding Act, which was meant to improve the country's economy. The Gibson Inn reopened in 1985. The restoration of one of the pillars of downtown Apalachicola was a turning point in the town's revitalization.

Today, the Gibson Inn at Market Street and Avenue C is one of the buildings on the Federal Register of Historic Places that still operates as a full-service facility. It is a particular favorite among tourists who want to see the "old Florida" and who like the building's two decks of wraparound porches with their wicker chairs, the cupola, and widow's walk with a spyglass. Each of the inn's thirty-one rooms is different in size, shape, color, and furnishings reminiscent of the Victorian era, but all are equipped with modern baths, telephone, and cable TV. The inn offers entertaining activities for its guests, including a favorite among visitors: Murder Mystery Weekends, which involves the solving of a crime on the premises. The 1994 book *America Restored* features the Gibson Inn as one of two sites in Florida worthy of attention and praise for the care its owners have taken to restore it to its former grandeur.

Coombs House Inn. This elegant Victorian mansion at Highway 98 and Sixth Street is a bed-and-breakfast that offers the charm and historical authenticity of another era in a homelike atmosphere. James Coombs was a Republican from Maine who fought for the Union and migrated to Apalachicola after the Civil War. In the early 1880s, he established in town a sawmill and store and then joined with another Northerner, Charles Parlin, to establish what became the Franklin County Lumber Company. While Parlin moved to Carrabelle, where the company had its sawmill, Coombs stayed in Apalachicola, where he prospered in business and banking. One of the boats that ran between Apalachicola and Pensacola was named the *James N. Coombs*.

For the large home he wanted for his family in Apalachicola in 1905, he chose one of the town's best builders, George H. Marshall. The style of the house is Queen Anne; it has an ornate staircase and veranda, a striking reception room, black cedar walls, a beamed ceiling, and an oak staircase. The three-story house, which is crowned by a widow's walk, has ten guest rooms and nine fireplaces.

The house sat vacant for many years, boarded up and uninviting. Then, in 1982, designer Lynn Wilson and her husband, Bill Spohrer, visited Apalachicola for the first time. They discovered the house in the historic district near the waterfront, realized its architectural significance, and spent the next seven years trying to buy it. They finally succeeded in 1992. They then spent two years restoring the Victorian mansion, which they named after the original owner. Today, the grounds surrounding the stately yellow mansion have tall palms and moss-draped oak trees.

The house has ten rooms, all with their own private bath. Guests particularly like the very wide front door leading into an impressive entryway and a hall with an original hand-carved oak staircase. The hall has recess-paneled black cypress walls and a beamed ceiling with floors of tiger oak. The master bedroom, which once was Mr. Coombs's special room, today has a king-size, four-poster bed and its own private Jacuzzi tub. In the backyard is Camellia Hall, which is used for weddings, meetings, and receptions.

The Coombs House actually consists of two residences: the Main House (built in 1905) and, just eighty steps away, Coombs House East (built in 1911). The homes have many antiques, oil paintings and beautiful carpets from around the world.

The Flatauer House. What today is the office of Gulf State Bank at 73 Avenue E can be traced back to Adolf Flatauer, a German Jewish merchant and immigrant. When he decided to build a large home for his large family in his new town of Apalachicola around 1908, he had local architect/builder George Marshall build it in what is still in the center of the town's historical district. The eight main rooms measure seventeen by seventeen and have a glazed fireplace and bay window in each. The downstairs library and dining room have sliding double doors made of dark wood. The staircase to the second floor is decorated with scrolled brackets. The house, which has over five thousand square feet of living space, also boasted indoor bathrooms, a rarity in much of America at the time.

In 1919, Mrs. Flatauer died in the terrible post–World War I flu epidemic. The following year, Mr. Flatauer, who never recovered from the death of his wife, committed suicide in the house. In the 1920s, workers made some additions to the rear of the house, which was converted to apartments. In the next six decades, the house deteriorated until it became an eyesore.

When Gulf State Bank acquired the building, its officials resolved to restore the once-elegant house, although they had only one old photograph on which to base the reconstruction. Workers restored it in 1980, putting wood shingles on the roof and restoring the widow's walk and the two-story porches with porch railings with hundreds of spindles. This carefully restored former residence is a good example of how historically minded businesses can convert homes into tasteful office buildings.

The Henry Brash House at 67 Avenue D, also known as The Porches, is the only site in Franklin County on Florida's Jewish Heritage Trail. Henry Brash, a native of Germany who served as a Confederate soldier, moved to Apalachicola in 1865, built the house that now bears his name, and worked as a merchant and sponge fisherman for forty years. He and his wife, Henrietta, raised their eleven children in this house. According to the booklet produced by the Florida Department of State, *Jewish Heritage Trail*, they "*kashered* (ritually cleansed) their dishes in the Gulf of Mexico and held Passover *Seder* dinners on the beach." The porches, which give the house its nickname and which wrap around the house on both levels, were added in 1890. The kitchen is built around a brick arch that was constructed of old, handmade bricks. Henry Brash was succeeded by one of his sons, who ran several stores in what came to be known as Brash's Block in Apalachicola.

The Marks/Clark House at the corner of Highway 98 and Fifth Street may be the oldest home in Apalachicola, having been brought to the town from Port St. Joe along with another dozen houses in the early 1800s. Workers barged and then reassembled the house, which may have been moved from Port St. Joe after a yellow fever epidemic decimated the town's population; a hurricane and tidal wave finished off what was left of the town. The two-story structure with thirty-six hundred square feet of living space was also known as the Marks/Bruce House from some early owners of the house and may have been constructed of wood from an eighteenth-century sailing vessel. The building with its four bedrooms, three baths, original hardware floors, and five fireplaces has been renovated into commercial/residential use.

These five houses, which have been carefully restored and brought up to modern safety standards, represent the growing trend of restoring buildings rather than tearing them down for building new ones.

20.

CHURCHES

"Whatever its reputation for wickedness

Apalachicola had a number of churches."

—William W. Rogers and Lee Willis, III, *At the Water's Edge*

WHILE THE CHURCHES OF APALACHICOLA represent different denominations and time periods, five in particular stand out for their history and significance.

Trinity Episcopal Church is the oldest. The congregation dates back to 1836, when local Episcopalians began holding services in Apalachicola. When the congregation decided to build a church, a lack of local skilled labor and materials forced them to go to White Plains, New York, to buy a structure. The white-pine building, which is on the National Register of Historic Places, was shipped in sections from New York and brought up around Florida through the Gulf of Mexico to Apalachicola. Workers assembled the Greek Revival–style building with wooden pins in 1838. Officials claim that the church is the sixth oldest one in Florida, the second oldest church still holding services, and possibly the first prefabricated structure in Florida.

Among the notable architectural features are the double hand-worked entrance columns, ornate wood ceiling, dark woodwork, beautiful colored windows depicting the Holy

Trinity Episcopal Church, which is on the National Register of Historic Places, was shipped in sections from New York and brought up around Florida through the Gulf of Mexico to Apalachicola in 1838.

Family and Apostles, and rare Erben Tracker organ from the 1840s. Also on the grounds is a Victorian-style parsonage that dates back to 1900. In 1932, the congregation added Benedict Hall, which is a parish house, Sunday school building, meeting place, and fellowship hall named after the late Reverend George Benedict, who was minister at Trinity from 1916 until 1930.

On the back wall of the church visitors can see paintings and photographs of the early church, rectory, and nearby square. Before the Civil War, blacks heard the same sermons as whites, but had separate pews in the balcony. During the Civil War, the original bell of the church was melted down to make a cannon, and the church's cushions and rugs were used for blankets and clothing. Among the church's early members were inventor/physician Dr. John Gorrie and botanist Dr. Alvan Chapman.

This particular church was where a local resident, Winifred Kimball, claims she got the inspiration to write a short story entitled "In Newness of Life," which won the ten-thousand-dollar grand prize in a 1922 contest held by the *Chicago Daily News*. The story was made into a Goldwyn Picture Corporation seven-reel motion picture, *Broken Chains*, which had its world premiere at the Dixie Theatre in Apalachicola on January 1, 1923.

Each May, Trinity hosts a Historic Tour of Homes that features some of the town's most architecturally significant buildings. See Visitor Information for details.

The **First United Methodist Church** stands at 75 Fifth Street. The Methodists of Apalachicola began holding their services in 1839, but did not officially organize until 1844. At first, members met in each other's homes or shared the new Episcopal church. In 1846, they spent thirty-five hundred dollars to build a new structure on Apalachicola's main street. That building became the site of meetings of the local Temperance Society around 1845 as they made plans to curtail the townspeople's alcoholic consumption. The original church building was destroyed by a 1900 fire which also razed much of the town, but the congregation rebuilt the structure on the same site.

The building, with its original belfry ladder, has eighteen gothic windows whose designs emphasize nature. The inside of the building has a central chandelier and fluted lighting fixtures. A stained-glass window in the church entitled "Apalachicola Orange Blossoms: 1899–1900" portrays citrus growers around the turn of the nineteenth century, when weather conditions were more conducive to growing citrus. The parsonage next door was built in the early 1900s and has served the church's pastors and families ever since. Its Victorian design is known for its intricate gingerbread work.

The **St. Paul African Methodist Episcopal (AME) Church** at I Avenue and Sixth Street is on the National Register of Historic Places. The congregation was organized in 1866, right after the Civil War, when members bought the land on which the church stands. They recorded the church's name on the deed as "Methodist Episcopal Church for Colored People." Soon afterwards, the congregation built a small, wooden building there, which served them for seventy-four years. In 1874, the church changed its name to St. Paul African Methodist Episcopal Church and became affiliated with the AME Church, which had been founded in Philadelphia in 1816.

The present large, red brick structure is the third one on the site, dating back to 1921. The building is known for its two brick towers with their metal steeples, peaked Gothic windows at the front, and stained-glass windows throughout that were made in Germany especially for St. Paul's. Since then, fire has struck the structure twice, but it has been rebuilt each time.

The first Catholics in the area were the Spanish explorers of the sixteenth century, who did not stay long. The local Catholic congregation dates back to 1845, when Reverend Timothy Birmingham organized the local Catholics and served them along with other missions in North Florida and South Georgia.

The first wooden facility of **St. Patrick's Roman Catholic Church** was built in 1850 but burned down the same year. It was rebuilt two years later and served local Irish, Italian, and other ethnic groups. That building, which was moved to where the priest's house is located today, was replaced by a new building around 1928 at the corner of Avenue C and

Sixth Street. It has the bells from the 1850 facility.

The congregation built the structure in a Romanesque style. Its main entrance has ornate stonework and recessed arches. The high-ceilinged structure is balanced by buttresses on the north and south sides, and the roof tiles give the church a Spanish look. The church building at 27 Sixth Street was restored and rededicated in 1994 and remains one of the town's most distinctive landmarks.

A statue of St. Patrick is located on the front of the white structure, just above a round stained glass window. The interior has a lavishly decorated confessional, as well as round brass chandeliers hanging over the wooden pews. Altars are dedicated to the Blessed Virgin and St. Joseph, and statues honor such saints as St. Patrick and St. Martin de Porres.

The local white Baptists organized themselves into a congregation in 1848. At first, they had allowed African Americans to join them in services, but, as the African Americans outnumbered their white neighbors, the two groups began their own churches. The **First Baptist Church** at 46 Ninth Street has its original brass-lock fixture on the front door. The original church, built around 1850 on the corner of Sixth Street and Avenue H, was repaired and reorganized in 1885. The present church was built in 1902, and its name was changed to Calvary Baptist Church. The new name lasted until 1934, when the church once again became First Baptist Church.

The white wooden tower at one corner of the building resembles a prayer tower. The theater-in-the-round style of the inside is impressive as it slopes down to the sanctuary. The interior walls have veneered woodwork, and the gothic windows are multicolored.

Florida frontier towns on the northern Gulf of Mexico such as St. Joseph and Apalachicola sometimes had a bad reputation, no doubt fueled by visiting sailors looking for a good time. The town's churches struggled to overcome that reputation and succeeded to some extent. The town's *Commercial Advertiser* newspaper, on April 11, 1846, encouraged the teetotalers to be strong in their resolve: "God give them the strength of resolution to resist the temptations they must encounter! Ice, sugar, wine, and Madeira!"

21.

SCHOOLS

"Tate's Hell State Forest Money Heaven-sent"

—*The Apalachicola Times* headline, March 29, 2001

T IMBER SALES AND RECREATION FEES FROM Tate's Hell State Forest have provided badly needed income for the schools of Franklin County. The Department of Agriculture and Consumer Services, Division of Forestry, returns fifteen percent of the revenue obtained from timber harvests, recreation, and other incoming-producing services in Tate's Hell State Forest to Franklin and Liberty Counties. Franklin County uses that money for its schools.

Soon after the town of Apalachicola was founded in 1831, the townspeople established some of the infrastructure that still exists today, including a newspaper, local ordinances, and schools. One of the private schools was the Apalachicola Academy, which Samuel Bryan and a female assistant (whose name is unknown) opened in 1848. In that school, boys and girls attended classes in separate rooms for two terms of twenty-two weeks each. Because local schools were private, some of the students went to other towns for their education. Just before the Civil War broke out, Franklin County had four schools, which had four teachers, served 182 students, and was financed by local taxation. In those days, only whites could attend schools, and the majority of white youngsters did.

Apalachicola's Chapman High School, named after local botanist Dr. Alvan Chapman, traces its beginnings to around

Because Franklin County is so large, school buses have been transporting children to the different schools for years.

1898, when several wooden buildings at the corner of Twelfth Street and Avenue E served the local students. A new brick three-story high school on the same site replaced the wooden school in 1915 at a cost of twenty-six thousand dollars. In 1933, two floors and an auditorium were added to the building, and the 1915 building was covered with slabs of stone and concrete in order to match the new one. The school acquired an industrial arts department in 1936, a high school band in 1939, a school orchestra in 1940, and a new gymnasium in 1941. In 1940, the faculty organized a student government and the school's first newspaper, *The Chapman Shark*. The Chapman Auditorium, one of the oldest buildings in North Florida, was built between 1929 and 1934 in the Egyptian Revival–Art Deco period architecture. Although the auditorium had poor acoustics, it could seat four hundred people. Today it is on the National Register of Historic Places, along with several rooms in Chapman High School.

During World War II, Apalachicola schools suffered from a lack of supplies and teachers as well as deteriorating buildings that could not be fixed. They had so few students during the war that Chapman had to have irregular schedules and reduce its football squad to six. After World War II, the 1915 Chapman building was demolished and replaced by several one-story buildings. Later, those buildings were demolished to make room for the state's first solar energy school, Chapman Elementary School, which was finished in 1979. The solar energy did not work adequately and caused many arguments in the county about how to deal with it.

Chapman High School served only white students since segregation of the races was in effect until late 1968. African Americans were able to attend their own school after the Civil War partly because of the efforts of Emmanuel Smith. Smith, a free black who could read and write and later served as Apalachicola's postmaster (1881–1886), was appointed to the Franklin County School Board in 1869 and served on the board until he died in 1886. After he convinced the school board to build a school for African Americans, the board hired Ezekiel Walton, a minister at the St. Paul A.M.E. Church, to build the "Colored School" for $250. In the

1890s, the school's name was changed to the Paul Laurence Dunbar School to honor the first African-American (1872–1906) to gain national eminence as a poet. Paul Laurence Dunbar School was located at the north end of Eighth Street; the main building and playground were between Eighth and Ninth Streets.

One of Dunbar's first principals, Gaddis C. Hall, was a graduate of Tallahassee's Florida Agricultural and Mechanical College (FAMU) who took great pride in running the school and in keeping its physical grounds as picturesque as possible. The school's seven teachers taught grades one through nine. In 1934, the remaining high school years were added. Before then, parents had had to send their children to schools in Marianna, Quincy, and Tallahassee to complete their education. In 1936, the school had its first graduating class, made up of twelve students.

After the school burned down in 1943 because of a defective flue, African Americans held classes in the Masonic and Odd Fellows Halls located in what became known as "The Hill" around Seventh and Eighth Streets. Wallace M. Quinn, the white owner of a local menhaden plant, donated twenty-one acres for a new high school, which was appropriately named after him and was finished in April, 1945. Despite Quinn's generosity, the facilities at that school were still, unfortunately, inferior to those at the white high school. Although Quinn High School no longer exists, one of its buildings still stands, a brick storage building behind the new high school. Dr. Frederick Humphries, who went on to become president of FAMU in Tallahassee in 1985 is a former graduate of Quinn High School. Alumni from the Quinn School have an annual reunion at Apalachicola's Seafood Festival.

The Civil Rights Act of 1964 forced school districts in the South to implement the very slowly developing concept of integration that the 1954 Brown decision by the U.S. Supreme Court had established. The races were integrated in Franklin County in 1968 with relatively few problems. For example, an African American student was elected student-body president of Carrabelle High School two years later.

Apalachicola High School had its first African-American principal, Vera Banks, in 2002; Chapman Elementary had Rose McCoy in 1981. Several African Americans are among the teachers with the longest service at Dunbar and Quinn High Schools: Louise Baker (46 years of teaching), Maude Collins (22 years), Mary Edwards (42 years), Gladys Ford (36 years), Ruby Tampa (41 years), Mary Tolliver (46 years), Olivia Woods (36 years), and Maude Wynn (37 years).

Despite its relatively few students, Apalachicola High School has distinguished itself in several ways. For example, its Student Council won first place among similarly sized schools, based on criteria like student-faculty relations, school spirit, fundraising, membership motivation and development, citizenship development, school service, and community service. The Student Council continued winning first place for the next several years.

One of Eastpoint's first buildings was a school. When new settlers moved there from Georgia in the 1890s, having floated down the Apalachicola River on two thirty-foot-long house barges, they dismantled the barges to build the first houses and a small schoolhouse, where Miss Josephine Wine from Virginia taught the children.

In the 1890s, the lighthouse keepers on Little St. George Island hired a teacher for their eleven children because of the difficulty of crossing the bay twice a day to attend school in Apalachicola. The first public school graduation on the mainland occurred in 1898. One of the male students refused to attend because girls were participating.

Carrabelle has its own high school, a facility that dates back to another building built in 1928–1929 in the center of town. Charles Watson, who spent fifteen years teaching math and science at Wallace M. Quinn High School, became the only black teacher at Carrabelle High School when integration brought the races together in Franklin County; Watson spent thirty-eight years teaching in the county schools. In 1971, the school was decommissioned and sold to a developer, who demolished it to make way for a shopping center. A new high school was eventually built to serve the students east of the Apalachicola River in Franklin County.

The athletic fields at some of Apalachicola's schools honor local citizens. For example, the baseball field at Apalachicola High School is named Jimmy Bloodworth Field in honor of a local man who played professional baseball for eleven years from 1937 to 1951. Bloodworth played in 1,002 games, hit sixty-two homers, and had a .248 lifetime batting average while playing for the Washington Senators, Detroit Tigers, Pittsburgh Pirates, Cincinnati Reds, and Philadelphia Phillies.

Bloodworth left another mark in the town he grew up in. In 1947, when he began playing baseball for the Pittsburgh Pirates, he met one of the owners of the Tigers, singer Bing Crosby. When Crosby found out that his new ball player was from a place called Apalachicola, Crosby took out a map, saw other place names like Panama City, Ochlockonee, and Tallahassee, and remarked that those names could be part of some ear-catching lyrics. The resulting song, "Apalachicola, Florida," appeared in the opening scene of his 1947 movie with Bob Hope, *Road To Rio*. Although the song never made the top twenty, it did make the town well known to many and was adopted by the Apalachicola baseball team in 1948. During the first months of that season, the song was played before the start of each game in honor of Bloodworth.

The football field at Apalachicola High School honors William "Pop" Wagoner, who coached many Sharks to football victories in thirty-two uninterrupted years, including a 12–0 season and the state championship in 1968. He finally retired in 1981. The Lady Sharks softball field is named Bill Martina Field in honor of a man who coached the girls' team for five years in the 1980s with his wife, Burnell.

The Willie Speed Building on the grounds of Apalachicola High School honors another man long associated with that school. Willie Burghart Speed earned his degree in Industrial Arts from FAMU after World War II, taught in Ocala for two years, returned to Franklin County to work, and later served as principal of the all-black Quinn High School (1954–1968), which taught grades kindergarten through twelfth. After the schools were integrated in 1968, he worked in the district office. He retired from the school system in 1992 and then served two terms on the school board, finally retiring in 2000.

From time to time, a local committee recommends that Franklin County make one of the two existing high schools into a middle school for grades six through eight and then consolidate the student bodies of the two present high schools into one to be located midway between Apalachicola and Carrabelle. Nothing has come of that, probably because the traditions associated with each school are too strong to overcome.

Two Catholic elementary schools existed in Apalachicola in the early part of the twentieth century—Our Lady, Star of the Sea School for white students and Holy Family Catholic School for black students. The former, taught by the Sisters of Mercy, opened in 1901 in a building near the Apalachicola River that burned down in 1929 but was rebuilt the following year. The school closed in 1950 because of a lack of teachers and funds, although the nuns did operate a summer religious vacation school until 1962. The latter school operated from 1922 until 1968. The building later served as a center providing food and clothing to the less fortunate.

The Apalachicola Bay Charter (ABC) School is a free, performance-based school that opened in 2001 at the Apalachicola Community Center in Battery Park. The school opened with sixty-two students and plans on adding more students and grades each year. In 2002, it moved to a site at the end of Fred Meyer Street on eleven acres donated by the St. Joe Timber Company.

The Anneewakee School in the Carrabelle area, officially called Anneewakee-on-the-Gulf, was a private school for troubled boys, but it has been closed for some time now. (The word *Anneewakee* was a Native American one meaning "land of the friendly people.")

Finally, one local man who succeeded in life through education was Kenneth Montgomery (1903–1996), who left Apalachicola with the help of an uncle, attended good schools and colleges, became a Chicago lawyer, and financed many college scholarships to deserving youngsters, especially minority students; he also worked to encourage law-school graduates to pursue public interest careers.

22.

PARKS AND CEMETERIES

Apalachicola was chosen as "the first site in the nation

to receive permission to duplicate the Three Servicemen

Statue" because the town "is representative of the many

small Southern towns that were home for large numbers

of Vietnam service members.

—*The Apalachicola Times*, September 27, 2001

THE LAYOUT OF APALACHICOLA IS BASED on that of Philadelphia, Pennsylvania. The one-square-mile grid in the central part of town has rectangular blocks complete with an open square at each of the four corners (Chapman, Franklin, Gorrie, and Madison), then a larger town square in the middle. In theory, the imposition of the so-called Philadelphia Plan on Apalachicola would cause the town to expand out from the center, but early decision-makers failed to take into consideration the importance of the river and bay to commercial development. The town developed, not in ever-expanding circles from the squares, but out from the river to the west. Two of Apalachicola's three parks (Battery and Lafayette) are near the bay.

PARKS

Battery Park. After the Apalachicola Land Company obtained clear title to the Apalachicola area in 1835, it began laying out the town with wide streets in the commercial area

Many weddings and picnics are held in the white gazebo in Lafayette Park.

as well as two parks and several squares. Planners thought that residents would build their homes around the squares and that it would expand slowly outward. Instead, early residents built their homes near the waterfront either to take advantage of the proximity to their sea-related businesses or because of the beauty of the offshore scenery. You can still find houses along Fifth Street that date back to the 1830s and 1840s.

Several civic-minded citizens, however, were determined to build the planned parks anyway. One of those people, John Ruge, was a major businessman in Franklin County in the late 1800s, involved in oyster-gathering and real estate. Before he died in 1931, he deeded to the city of Apalachicola some of his land on what became known as Battery Park and Battery Park Basin between Fourth and Sixth Streets.

Mr. and Mrs. J.P. Hickey were also important in the development of the park. Their house was at the intersection of Avenue B and Fourth Street. Mrs. Hickey, who wanted a park in front of their house for all to enjoy, led community efforts in leveling the hilly land and spreading excess topsoil over the marshy area to create more land. Officials obtained eight Civil War cannons from a fort near Pensacola and put them in the park, thus the name Battery Park. When America entered World War I, six of the cannons were used in the war effort, leaving behind some cannon balls and two cannons, which were mounted on cement pillars.

During World War II, in order to accommodate servicemen's families who wanted to be near them before they were shipped overseas after they had finished training at places like Camp Gordon Johnston, local officials built restrooms with showers in Battery Park. Families with trailers were able to keep them in the park; one family, unable to procure local housing, lived in a Boy Scout hut in the park.

When local officials planned to build a new community center in Battery Park in 1992, archaeologists had to do the usual state-mandated analysis of the site. They found remnants of several different Native American cultures who had lived there thousands of years ago. Evidence pointed to the presence of Native Americans from A.D. 1,000 to the time the Spanish arrived in the sixteenth century. To honor those Native

Americans, local officials had representatives of several tribes, for example the Cherokee, Seminole, and Creek, to bless the site of the community center in 1993. At that time, Chief Medicine Wolf Ross Nowling called upon the Great Spirit and Mother Earth Natasha to give their blessings to the site.

The community center that was eventually built there with funds from the Florida Department of Community Affairs and that has served as a meeting room and as a charter school building is built on pilings thirteen feet above sea level.

Among the festivities held in Battery Park each year is the Seafood Festival, which attracts over twenty thousand people. The Boy Scouts, especially Apalachicola Troop No. 140 and St. George Island Troop No. 22, have many of their activities in the park's Scout house, which was built by Herbert Marshall in 1946.

The park also has two well-placed boardwalks that extend out over the water. The basin has a public boat ramp. The site, known officially as Battery Point Marina, used to be called, at different times, Ten Foot Hole, the City Marina, and the Apalachicola Boat Basin. Boats are important in Apalachicola for their use in commerce, but also more and more for taking visitors around the bay. The *Jubilee* is a paddle boat on which a guide describes the history of the area in terms of its Native Americans, cotton industry, and fishing. Other tour boats stress eco-tourism.

The pride of the boat fleet was the *Governor Stone*, a floating National Historic Landmark dating back to Mississippi in 1877. Made of cypress and juniper wood, the sixty-three-foot-long gaff-rigged schooner, which the local Apalachicola Maritime Institute brought from Mississippi in 1990, once transported cargo, but later carried passengers around the bay and helped teach maritime history.

The authentic, carefully restored *Governor Stone* is the oldest sailing vessel in Florida, although its origins are elsewhere. Charles Greiner of Pascagoula, Mississippi, built the schooner in 1877 as a cargo freighter and named it for a friend, John Marshall Stone, the first elected governor of Mississippi after the Civil War. The schooner has been used as an oyster boat, rumrunner, sponge freighter, training vessel, yacht club committee boat, and pleasure craft. In World War II, the U.S. Merchant Marine used it for anti-submarine patrols. Its shallow draft and huge amount of sail allow it to pass over the many sand bars along the Gulf Coast before deep channels were dug. The *Stone* has sunk twice and been beached twice by hurricanes, but has survived to be the last such schooner still sailing. In 2003, Walton County's Eden State Gardens bought the schooner and had it shipped there for use as an exhibit.

Lafayette Park, on Avenue B at the south end of 14th Street in the western part of town, was designated a city park in 1832. Its name honors the Marquis of Lafayette, an early friend of the United States. It used to have a cemetery, which is now closed. In the late nineteenth century, when the local timber industry was thriving, residents built large homes along the nearby Bay Avenue to take advantage of the beautiful view and the park. The park provides spectacular views of those beautiful Victorian-style homes as well as the bay and distant islands.

The park used to have a pier that joined with a boardwalk running between this park and Brown's Pier at Battery Park. It provided residents a space to promenade. A 1920s hurricane destroyed it, turning a white, sandy beach, which used to extend between the two parks and stretched ten to thirty feet in width, into a marshy area. Today, the pier, which extends about nine hundred feet into the marsh and waters of the Gulf, has a T-shaped recreation dock.

In 1992, the City of Apalachicola and the Historic Apalachicola Foundation restored the park, adding a white gazebo, brick walkways around the many live oak trees, period lightposts, flower gardens, children's play equipment, picnic tables, and barbecue grills. Local architect Willoughby Marshall helped design many of the park's features such as the gazebo, the shrubs, flowers, and live oaks that have made it a favorite among residents and visitors alike. Open-air concerts and weddings are held there.

A nearby home, at 15 13th Street on the northeast corner across from the park, was the home of novelist Alexander Key (1904–1979), author of such novels as *The Wrath and the Wind* (1949) and *Island Light* (1950), both of which take place in Apalachicola. Originally called Villa Rosa, the mustard-colored house with the gingerbread design has been carefully restored to its former splendor.

This might be a good place to mention three other local writers. Peggy Bennett wrote the novel *Varmints* (1946) about the lives of natives in a small Florida Gulf coastal town named Tupelo. Jim Fergus is the author of the nonfiction *A Hunter's Road: A Journey with Gun and Dog Across the American Uplands* (1993) and the fictional *One Thousand White Women—The Journals of May Dodd* (1999). Teresa Holloway (1906–1989), who was born in Apalachicola, graduated from the Florida State College for Women (later Florida State University), and worked as manager of the town's chamber of commerce from 1947 to 1950. She published thirty-nine novels under her own name as well as the pen names Elizabeth Beatty and Margaret Vail McLeod. Her *Heart's Haven* (New York: Avalon, 1955) is set in Apalachicola.

Veterans Memorial Park. The Apalachicola City Commission approved plans in 2001 for a Veterans Park on Water Street. The park may become the site of the first replica of the Vietnam veterans' Three Servicemen Statue at the Vietnam Veterans Memorial in Washington, D.C. Apalachicola was chosen because it is a good representative of many small Southern towns that supplied soldiers for the Vietnam War and because the founder of the Vietnam Veterans Memorial Fund (VVMF), Jan Scruggs, served in that war with Franklin County Commissioner Jimmy Mosconis, who has actively supported the location of the replica statue in Apalachicola.

CEMETERIES

Chestnut Street Cemetery. The placement of cemeteries in a new settlement is an important decision. They should be in a quiet place away from the path of development, but not too far from the churches and homes of people who want to pay their respects to the departed on a regular basis. Because subsequent generations do not usually want to disturb cemeteries by, for example, reburying the dead to make way for construction, planners usually take great care in the initial location.

When Apalachicola beat its bitter nearby rival, St. Joseph, as the main port in that part of Florida in the 1830s, the Apalachicola Land Company, which owned much of the land, began selling lots, first to the local residents, and then to outsiders. In preparation for the sales, the company laid out Apalachicola's streets carefully, established several parks for public use, and set aside land for a cemetery.

The town's oldest cemetery, Chestnut Street Cemetery was begun in 1831 and was named at first the Old City Graveyard. The site reflects the history of the town since it is the final resting place of Confederate soldiers who fought in the Civil War, victims of shipwrecks off the coast, children lost to childhood diseases, even whole families that died from yellow fever.

Interred there are some of the town's founders and early residents, including botanist Dr. Alvan Chapman, who died in 1899, and his wife. Of particular note are several dozen family plots with elaborate black-iron work surrounding the headstones. The Daughters of the Confederacy place miniature Confederate flags at the sites of the former Confederate soldiers buried here and in Magnolia Cemetery. Visitors driving along Highway 98 (Avenue E) can see the cemetery between Sixth and Eighth Streets.

The cemetery, which has over five hundred graves, has been carefully mapped by the Church of Latter Day Saints as part of the church's extensive genealogical work. The upkeep of the site is often done by local residents who have lived there for decades and who feel strongly about tending the gravesites of long-lost friends.

Magnolia Cemetery. Magnolia Cemetery, in the northwest section of town, replaced a site near Lafayette Park in the southwestern section of the city where many early settlers were buried. When the land near Lafayette Park became valuable because of its location, officials moved the remains in that cemetery to Magnolia Cemetery. Among the many people buried in Magnolia Cemetery are Herbert Smith, who—after being listed twenty-two years as Missing in Action (MIA) in the Vietnam War, was buried in 1988.

There are no doubt other cemeteries in the area, but time and neglect have taken their toll on such sites. As archaeologists do diggings in the bay area, they will probably come upon such cemeteries. For example, the Snowhill Cemetery, which is outside the city limits, is where many African Americans were buried, although the records of who was buried there may be lost.

All in all, Apalachicola has done a good job in preserving its historic district and in controlling development. The Historic Apalachicola Foundation, Inc., which was organized in 1988 from an earlier group, the Citizens Advisory Committee, helped revive and implement the city's historic 1835 plan. In preserving its waterfront and keeping the small town squares around Apalachicola, the foundation has made the town appealing to tourists and yet able to expand to the north and west.

23.

JOHN GORRIE MUSEUM
AND CHAPMAN HOUSE

"In Statuary Hall in the nation's air-conditioned Capitol, one

of the two niches allotted to Florida is filled with a statue of

John Gorrie, physician, scientist, inventor."

— "John Gorrie: Physician, Scientist, Inventor,"

The Southern Medical Journal, December, 1935

EVERYONE WHO ENJOYS AN AIR-CONDITIONED facility today owes a large debt of gratitude to a soft-spoken, mild-mannered doctor from Apalachicola. Air-conditioning, along with mosquito control and highway construction, was one of the most important factors in the development of Florida in the twentieth century. And it all began in a little house in Apalachicola where a quiet, unassuming man transformed medicine and led to the great influx of visitors and residents to Florida in the twentieth century.

John Gorrie (1803–1855) was either born on the island of St. Nevis in the West Indies or, as a monument in Apalachicola says, in Charleston, South Carolina. He studied medicine at the College of Physicians and Surgeons of the Western District of New York from 1825 to 1827, practiced medicine in South Carolina from 1828 to 1833, and settled in Apalachicola in 1833. He earned part of his living by serving as postmaster of the growing town, and later, as a notary public and mayor. His background is somewhat mysterious, and

John Gorrie's ice-making machine cooled the rooms of his malarial patients and led eventually to the invention of air conditioning.

certain years are unaccounted for. But in Florida during the nineteenth century, people did not really care or ask about someone's past, only what he could do in the present.

In 1838, Dr. Gorrie married Caroline Frances Myrick Beman, the widowed owner of the town's Florida Hotel. He and his wife then left the town for two years, but returned in 1840, just before Gorrie was named the local justice of the peace and just before yellow fever devastated the area. Dr. Gorrie became an important member of his community, serving in various organizations as a member, then chairman of the city council, treasurer of the city, postmaster, mayor, secretary of the Masonic Lodge, part-owner of the Mansion House Hotel, president of the Apalachicola Branch Bank of Pensacola, charter member of the Marine Insurance Bank of Apalachicola, founding vestryman of the town's Trinity Episcopal Church, and physician for the Marine Hospital Service of the U.S. Treasury Department. But something else began to absorb his attention, so much so that he resigned the coveted position of mayor to work full-time on it.

For centuries people believed that miasma or "swamp gas" caused such diseases as malaria and yellow fever. Because so many people, including doctors, believed that decaying vegetation in damp places caused malaria and yellow fever, they promoted the practice of draining and then filling in swamps and marshlands. What they did not realize was that mosquitoes, not the decaying vegetation of the swamps, spread the diseases. The Apalachicola Bay area has many swamps and tidal flats, areas that are ripe for mosquitoes. Dr. Gorrie probably came to realize how deadly mosquitoes are in spreading disease when he noticed that persons who slept under nets or lived on drained lands did not contract the diseases; he therefore urged the draining of surrounding swamps to rid the area of weeds where mosquitoes breed.

Doctors could treat malaria with quinine, but Dr. Gorrie wanted to try other methods as well. He came to believe that, if he could lower the room temperature of his malarial patients, he could possibly reduce the severity of the disease and at least make them more comfortable. In a series of articles written under the pen name of "Jenner" (in honor of

Edward Jenner, the discoverer of the smallpox vaccine), Gorrie began writing about the benefits of refrigeration for sick patients. In 1848, he submitted a petition for a patent on his refrigeration device, which produced blocks of artificial ice and which he had built in Cincinnati, Ohio, and had shipped to Apalachicola. In 1850, he received a British patent, and, the following year, a U.S. patent.

He had a lot of trouble when he sought money to back his invention. New England ice merchants, thinking that they would lose business, opposed him; others were skeptical about the efficacy of his ice machine. He found a financial backer in Massachusetts, but that person's premature death dried up Gorrie's funds. In the end, he received very little monetary return on his important breakthrough—in fact, he lost a good deal of money as well as his health in trying to promote the invention, and died unappreciated. Others falsely claimed that they had invented a "cooling" machine long after Gorrie had applied for his patent.

Even Willis Carrier, who built his first air-conditioner in New York in 1903, received more credit than the quiet man of Apalachicola. The world might never have even heard of Dr. Gorrie had his friend, fellow scientist Dr. Alvan Chapman, not spread the news of Gorrie's invention to scientific colleagues around the world.

When Dr. Gorrie died in 1855, he was first buried near the bay, in accordance with his final will, in which he had specified where he wanted to be buried: "I wish to be buried plainly and neatly, my body to be reposed in the public burial ground situated near the margin of the Bay of Apalachicola." Local officials later removed his body from near the beach when they realized that sand erosion was threatening the gravesite. Today he lies buried in the small park across from the Gorrie Museum.

Near Gorrie Square, the Municipal Library, and Trinity Episcopal Church is a monument honoring Dr. Gorrie. It was erected in the 1890s, when the brother of an acquaintance of Gorrie's who was in the ice business convinced other merchants to donate the proceeds of one ton of ice sold on July 4, 1897 to pay for the monument. Three years later local officials in Apalachicola dedicated that memorial, an obelisk that stands near the Gorrie Museum.

What is probably just as amazing as the lack of recognition Gorrie endured is the fact that his prediction that frozen foods and air conditioning would be common in ordinary homes took so long to come about. Not until after World War II did scientists finally develop methods to freeze food for shipments around the world. And it took a decade after that for ordinary people to afford air conditioning for their homes.

The Gorrie Museum features a replica of the doctor's ice machine (the original is in the Smithsonian Institution in Washington, D.C.). The museum has a portrait of Gorrie, probably the only one that exists. Dr. Gorrie's house, which burned down, may have been near the present-day armory at the corner of Fourth Street and D Avenue. His hospital, according to the park ranger at the Gorrie Museum, may have been behind the museum, but records from that era are incomplete.

A tree in front of the museum is known as the John Gorrie Red Cedar and is used in a program called America's Historic Forests, a series of learning centers that trace the heritage of this country through trees. The program collects seeds from trees that have a significant background, including the John Gorrie Red Cedar and a live oak directly across from the museum. Those seeds germinate and eventually join other trees that represent the history of the United States, including its presidents, their homes, famous battlefields, war heroes, statesmen, religious leaders, writers, inventors, and other famous people.

Dr. Gorrie is one of two Floridians honored in the Statuary Hall of Fame in the United States Capitol in Washington, D.C. (the other is General Edmund Kirby Smith of Civil War fame). Dr. Gorrie's name is also honored by the bridge linking Apalachicola with Eastpoint. In 2002, the Florida Secretary of State named him a "Great Floridian," an honor that recognized "his distinguished service to the citizens of the State of Florida and to our nation." "The Ice Man," a two-act play about Dr. Gorrie written by Eastpoint resident Tom Campbell, had its world premiere at

Apalachicola's Dixie Theatre in 2002.

World-famous botanist Dr. Alvan Chapman (1809–1899) is another well-known figure of nineteenth-century Apalachicola. Born of English parents and raised in Massachusetts, Dr. Chapman moved to Florida in the 1830s—first to Quincy to practice medicine, then to Marianna, and finally to Apalachicola in 1847. Although trained in medicine, once in Florida he became fascinated with the vast diversity of plants, began to study botany, and soon abandoned medicine for what turned out to be his real calling in life, despite the fact that he was color-blind. In 1860, he published *Flora of the Southern United States,* a significant work because for the next five decades it was the only and definitive catalogue of flowering plants in the southeastern United States. During the Civil War, his botanical collection trips around the Apalachicola area were restricted, but he remained in the town.

Living in the Southern town of Apalachicola during the Civil War must have caused Dr. Chapman some problems. A Northerner in many ways, he wanted the Union's victory, which annoyed his Southern wife so much that she returned to her home in Marianna, Florida (they were reconciled after the war). One wonders if Dr. Chapman's good friend, Dr. Gorrie, was also more sympathetic to the South and therefore the two learned men had arguments during the course of the war. Nonetheless, Dr. Chapman remained in the town he had come to love. He went on to not only produce the book that made him famous, but also to discover many plants species including Chapman's holly, Chapman's honeysuckle, and Chapman's rhododendron.

His presence in Apalachicola may have influenced another botanist, Asa Gray of Harvard University, to make the trip south in 1875 to see some of the botanical rarities that Dr. Chapman had written to him about. Dr. Gray, who became the leading authority of his time on the plant life of the United States, came to the Apalachicola Bluffs, a series of deep ravines along the Apalachicola River that was home to the very rare conifer with the Latin name *Torreya taxifolia* or "stinking cedar." Although not important economically to the area, the plant was the only known home of the stinking cedar.

Dr. Chapman served as a probate judge in Apalachicola, partly to pay the expenses of collecting botanical specimens. He continued working in Apalachicola and carrying on his important research until he died in 1899. He and his wife are buried in the Chestnut Street Cemetery off Highway 98.

Chapman House, the two-story, wooden white house that Dr. Chapman lived in, is just west of the Gulf State Bank on Highway 98 at Sixth Street. The house has a classical design. Originally, it had a central hallway on both floors with two rooms off each side of the hallway. The original kitchen was probably separated from the main house. In the early 1920s, William Popham, the self-declared "Oyster King," who had grandiose plans for developing Apalachicola and its nearby waters, bought the house and extensively remodeled it. Today, Chapman House is a privately owned office building.

Chapman High School honors Dr. Chapman as does the Chapman Botanical Gardens on North Market Street with its array of many different kinds of plants, including hollyhocks, crepe myrtle, and oleander. At the eight-acre garden, a board-walk over a swamp allows visitors to get a close view of a Florida marsh, and a gazebo and well laid-out patio enhance the beauty of the grounds.

It is remarkable that small, nineteenth-century Apalachicola was home to two such distinguished scientists. Clearly, the area offered opportunities to each man, not only for treating patients or collecting plant specimens, but also for living in very pleasant surroundings.

24.

AFRICAN AMERICANS IN APALACHICOLA

"You lived, died, and were buried on Seventh Street."

—a common saying among Apalachicola's African American

community to indicate how the street provided for the many

needs of those who lived there

AFRICANS AND AFRICAN AMERICANS HAVE PLAYED an important role in the history of Franklin County and Apalachicola Bay, especially as school desegregation of the 1960s and a tolerant attitude toward African Americans by the white community enabled the former to participate in school activities, hold political office, and run successful businesses in the county. Of the 11,057 residents of Franklin County in the 2000 census, 16.3 percent or 1,802 are African American, which is a higher percentage than the 14.6 percent for Florida as a whole.

One of the first non–Native Americans who may have arrived in this area is Estevanico the Black. He was enslaved after being captured in his homeland of Morocco. When his Spanish master decided to sign on with the 1528 expedition to the New World led by Pánfilo de Narváez, Estevanico became one of just a handful of survivors who sailed along the Florida coast in makeshift rafts from south of Tallahassee to Mexico.

The St. Paul African Methodist Episcopal Church on Sixth Street is a centerpiece of the African American community.

In the seventeenth and eighteenth centuries, African slaves played an important part in the economy of the South, including Florida, as they worked in cotton fields and rice plantations. Many of them escaped from the harsh conditions on those plantations and fled to freedom. In the late eighteenth and early nineteenth century, when Spain controlled the Florida peninsula, the United States complained that runaway slaves from Georgia and the Carolinas found refuge in the unsettled peninsula. That claim was just one of several that officials in the United States used to justify their encroachments into Spanish Florida.

Franklin County never had the large cotton plantations that other Southern counties had in the nineteenth century. Therefore, there were relatively few slaves in the county, a fact that would lessen the difficulties of integration in the 1960s. The slaves that did live in the county worked at labor-intensive jobs, for example on farms and possibly on boats. When they were freed after the Civil War, they were able to hire themselves out as laborers and earn money for their work.

In the eighteenth century, however, most African Americans in Franklin County and elsewhere did not learn how to read and write since customs and laws forbade such teaching. Even free blacks were restricted in their movements. In the 1830s, blacks who were caught in the town without the proper written passes could be punished with twenty strikes from a rawhide whip. It is remarkable that under such conditions, some slaves in Apalachicola were granted a measure of freedom and appreciation. For example, the history of Trinity Episcopal Church written by Jimmie J. Nichols, tells about a woman called Aunt Susan, a servant to the prominent Raney family. Back in the 1840s, the Raneys used to host a group that would make beautiful garments to benefit the Trinity Episcopal Church. Aunt Susan would take the finished products from house to house, selling them to the local housewives. When Aunt Susan died, she was interred in the Raney plot in Chestnut Cemetery.

Before the start of the Civil War in 1861, African Americans who were free, such as the sailors who frequented the port of Apalachicola working on American or foreign vessels, were not allowed to enter Apalachicola, but had to remain at a distance. During the Civil War, many residents of the town, including their slaves, left for more promising lands, especially because the Union blockade and obstructions placed in the Apalachicola River hurt the economy of the town.

When the Civil War ended in 1865, one of the Union troops occupying Apalachicola was the 82nd United States Colored Infantry under the command of Major General Alexander Asboth. In those difficult years after the war, many former slaves stayed on in Franklin County to raise their families and work at jobs for pay. Some of them were accepted into the community and took up positions of authority, such as a man named Frank, a former slave of the Cook family who took "Cook" for his last name and served for a time as a Vestryman of Trinity Episcopal Church.

During the Reconstruction Period after the Civil War, African Americans established St. Paul African Methodist Episcopal Church. By 1880 one of the two men on the police force in Apalachicola was black. African Americans operated several businesses in the area, including two of the main hotels in Apalachicola: the Spartan Jenkins, which served only whites, although it was run by African Americans; and the Fuller, which was run by Mary Aldin Fuller and her husband for about fifteen years, until she died in 1905. The Fuller Hotel eventually burned down in 1945.

A local African American, Emmanuel Smith, served on the Franklin County School Board during the Reconstruction Era after the Civil War and as the local postmaster from 1881 to 1885, to be replaced in the latter post at his retirement by the famous botanist, Dr. Alvan Chapman. Also during Reconstruction, the town had a black sheriff, Frank Hutchinson, who in turn had a black deputy, James Gulliam, who was sent to Jacksonville to bring back some prisoners but instead contracted yellow fever during the epidemic there, died, and was buried there.

When the twentieth century began, the local newspaper, *The Apalachicola Times,* had a column devoted to news of the local African-American community. One of the popular brass bands of the times was the Colored Odd Fellows, which performed in the early 1900s and which was the counterpart to the white band, the City Cornet Band. Many African Americans began attending St. Paul African Methodist Episcopal Church after it was built in 1913 (see chapter 20 for more about the church). Other sites of interest include the small cemetery on 12th Street and the one at the south end of Seventh Street, which safeguard the remains of many of Apalachicola's African-American ancestors.

During World War II, one of the first four draftees was an African American named Mose Langston. At Camp Gordon Johnston near Carrabelle many African American troops trained for amphibian landings, although the African American soldiers there were supplied with poor facilities and faced the Jim Crow segregation laws when they went on leave to Tallahassee.

When integration of facilities occurred in the 1960s as a result of the Civil Rights Act of 1964, the county experienced relatively few racial incidents, partly because Apalachicola did not have the sharp residential demarcation of the races that other towns had. While most African Americans lived in the northern section of town called "The Hill," whites also lived there, and other African Americans lived in other parts of the town. The Hill, so called because of the slight rise of the area from the surrounding streets, consisted of ten streets, from Fifth Street to 14th Street and from Highway 98 to Avenue M. Eight churches served the residents there from the early twentieth century until the present. Today, almost a thousand African Americans live there.

One of the buildings in town that an African American owned is the O.E. Cone Building at 67 Commerce Street. Constructed after the 1900 city fire, it once had a barbershop, laundry, and wood yard. A number of African-American clubs and fraternal organizations were active in Apalachicola during the twentieth century. The Odd Fellow Hall, located between avenues G and I on the left side of Sixth Street going south was the site of the Odd Fellow Lodge, a social organization, which had a woman's auxiliary named the Households of Ruth. The

Masonic Hall was located on Sixth Street between Avenues I and J going north on the right side of the street. Other similar organizations were the K of P (Knights of Pythias), Young Men's Progressive Club, Cream of the Crop, the Owl's Social Club, and the Social Lites. In 2000, African-American City Commissioner Robert Davis renamed Avenue J Martin Luther King Avenue to honor the civil rights leader.

Among the more famous local African Americans from Apalachicola is Frederick Humphries, who earned a Ph.D. in Physical Chemistry from the University of Pittsburgh and later became president of Tennessee State University and then Florida A&M University (FAMU) in Tallahassee. In 2001, he helped FAMU win a $2.5-million-per-year grant for three years from the National Oceanic and Atmospheric Administration (NOAA) to conduct research in Apalachicola Bay. After Dr. Humphries stepped down from the presidency of FAMU in 2001, he became the president of the National Association for Equal Opportunity in Higher Education. His sister, Mona, became school superintendent in Seattle, Washington.

Other local African Americans who went on to careers in educational administration include Willie Burghart Speed and his son, Oryan Speed. Willie served as principal of the all-black Quinn High School from 1954–1968, and later worked in the Apalachicola school district office. He is a great-grandson of Reconstruction-era Deputy Sheriff Gulliam mentioned earlier in the chapter. Oryan was a sixth-grade teacher at Brown Elementary School in Eastpoint before serving as an administrator in the Tampa school system in the 1990s.

Other prominent African Americans from the area who moved away to work are Dr. George Hilliard, a physician; William Kornegy, who became the Student Placement Director for General Motors; Mrs. Mattie Edwards Murrell, who became the Postal Inspector of New York City; Dr. Ben Sealey, the Director of Finances at Decatur Community College in Decatur, Georgia; and Charles Wilson, the vice-president of the Jim Walter Corporation.

Among the significant local African Americans in the last few decades are the following: Captain James Bunyon of the

Apalachicola Police Department; Jarred Burns Jr., principal of Chapman Elementary School, having replaced Rose McCoy (see below); Warren Hayward, president of the local chapter of the NAACP for several years and a member of the board of directors of the Community Action Program (CAP) that serves the poor of seven nearby counties; Azalee Johnson, one of the founders in 1969 of the NAACP and president of the organization for at least ten years; Rose McCoy, the first African American principal of Chapman Elementary School, the educator who replaced Willie Speed as District Administrator, also serving as finance commissioner of Apalachicola and owner-operator of a successful local monument company; Major Willie Norwood, commanding officer of Franklin Work Camp; Edward Tolliver, City Commissioner in Apalachicola in the 1970s and 1980s and then Franklin County Commissioner in the 1980s and 1990s. African Americans who have recently held political office in Apalachicola include city commissioners Robert Davis and Van Johnson.

Among the leaders in the African-American community are several people that should be mentioned: Vera Banks, the first African American principal of Apalachicola High School; John Croom, owner of a transportation business and travel agency in Apalachicola; Charles Jones Sr., president of the Hill Community Development Association, which worked hard to upgrade the buildings in the Hill area; Noah Lockley Sr., chairman of the Deacon Board of the Friendship Missionary Baptist Church who served on the Franklin County School Board in the 1990s and was active in community projects for over thirty-five years. Andy Williams was elected Apalachicola Police Chief in 1999, the first African American to hold that position.

A local African American, Dorothy Goosby, became her high school valedictorian in Apalachicola, went on to college, and moved to Long Island, New York, in the 1960s; she earned a master's degree in business, worked in nursing-home administration, and was elected to the governing board in Hempstead, New York, an accomplishment that made the *New York Times* (January 12, 2000).

Among the African-American visitors who have impacted the county is New York actress Saundra McClain, who spent a good part of 1982 teaching the county's youngsters about acting. She was an artist in residence who helped form a theater arts program.

Beginning around 2000, Apalachicola celebrated an annual African-American History Celebration sponsored by H'COLA (which stands for Hillside Coalition of Laborers of Apalachicola). The festivities include a parade, informational booths, and food vendors.

Many African Americans have succeeded as business people, educators, and civic leaders. Franklin County has succeeded in judging its citizens by their ability, not the color of their skin.

25.

MILITARY SITES

"The Army deliberately made the [Gordon Johnston]

camp primitive and dangerous to simulate the hardships

of fighting and to prepare the men for the horrors and

brutalities they would be facing on the battlefronts,

especially D-Day in June 1944."

—Marlene Womack, *War Comes to Florida's*

Northern Gulf Coast

UNLIKE MOST OTHER FLORIDA COUNTIES, Franklin County has a military history that involved a large percentage of its eligible soldiers and facilities. Military companies including the Alaqua Guards, City Cavalry, Apalachicola Guards, and City Dragoons made up an important part of early Apalachicola history. They defended the town, fought in the Seminole Indian wars, and provided their members a camaraderie and stepping stone into political office that other social groups did not.

After the Civil War began, the Apalachicola Guards of Franklin County became part of the First Florida Infantry, Company B. Young men enlisted for twelve months, confident that the war would soon be over and they could resume their lives. As military sentiment spread in Apalachicola, women gathered at the Raney House to design and sew a large regimental flag of white silk with the words "Apalachicola Guards" emblazoned at the top over seven stars that represented the first seven states to secede. That

The airfield two miles west of Apalachicola played a role in World War II.

flag was eventually returned to Florida and is displayed in Tallahassee's State Museum.

Local Confederate soldiers joined others at the Confederate arsenal up the river at Chattahoochee, then moved on to do battle in Pensacola. So few soldiers were left behind in Apalachicola during the war that it quickly fell to Union forces who set up a blockade in the bay in order to stop goods from entering and leaving the town.

By the time the Apalachicola Guards fought in Pensacola and later in Alabama, their year of enlistment was up. Of those men in Company B, forty reenlisted, while others joined other regiments later. They fought at such Civil War battles as Murfreesboro, Chickamauga, and Mission Ridge, as well as in other skirmishes in Tennessee and North Carolina. At the end of the war, only twenty-three men made it home from an initial roster of 930.

After the Civil War, the Union would not allow the South to have military organizations outside of the U.S. Army and Navy, but time would change that. Apalachicola's National Guard unit, the 106th Engineers, Company E, traces its history back to the Franklin Guards, a company of infantry organized in 1884 by J.H. Coombs and Fred Butterfield. It became part of the National Guard in 1890 and eight years later served in the Spanish-American War, after which it performed various duties at home such as keeping the peace and patrolling the area during storms.

The most obvious symbol of the military presence in Apalachicola is the Fort Coombs Armory, a huge, white brick building which dominates the corner of Fourth Street and D Avenue. Dating back to 1901 and named for Percy Coombs, an early active member of the local militia, the armory is one of only two owned by the State of Florida. Some historians believe that John Gorrie's house once stood where the armory's yard is today.

The building, with its arched, slit windows and four-story tower connected to it on the southeast corner, is the headquarters of the Franklin Guards, which date back to the Second Seminole War (1835–1842). Inside the arched portal is a cannon that was used during the Civil War to signal to

Confederate soldiers that the Union forces were approaching. The large main hall is used for town functions like high school proms.

During World War I, the county continued sending its citizens to serve their country. In that war, Franklin County was one of three counties in the United States that had more voluntary enlistments than were required in the nation's first two drafts. In that war, 248 men (174 whites and 74 blacks) volunteered to serve their country; that number represented nineteen percent of the men eligible for the draft in Franklin County.

In World War I, the Guard fought in Europe, including at the high-casualty battles in the Meuse-Argonne section of France. A local man who fought in that war, Willoughby Marks, is honored in the naming of the local American Legion Post and by a memorial in the plot of land in front of the Gibson Inn near the foot of the Gorrie Bridge. Marks fought in the Battle of the Argon Forest as company commander and senior first lieutenant. When he learned that one of his men was wounded and needed help, Marks went back to the aid of his fallen comrade and was killed in doing so. He was awarded the Distinguished Service Cross posthumously for his courage. Eleven other county youths also died in that war.

The Franklin Guards were discontinued after World War I, but regrouped in 1926. In November, 1940, the national guard unit was activated under the command of Captain Herbert Marshall (who would serve the county as sheriff after World War II), aided by Second Lieutenants W. Newt Creekmore Jr. and James Henry. The noncommissioned officers were First Sergeant Benjamin Bloodworth and Staff Sergeant Fred Richards.

In preparation for going overseas in World War II as part of the famous Dixie Division, Company E, 106th Engineers, the young soldiers would spend eight hours a day training at the armory. The armory was also used in 1942 to care for the fourteen survivors of HMS *Mica*, a British Liberty ship torpedoed by a German U-boat in the Gulf of Mexico twenty-five miles south of Apalachicola.

Apalachicola played a major part at Camp Gordon Johnston, which covered half of Franklin County and trained thousands of soldiers in the Amphibious Training Center, the country's only school for long-range, shore-to-shore operations (for more about Camp Gordon Johnston, see Chapter 16).

A plaque listing the names of the eighty individuals who served during World War II with the U.S. Army Corps of Engineers, Company E, 106th Division, was unveiled at the armory at a 1982 reunion. A star next to the name indicates that particular man died in war. Plaques on the outside wall commemorate the many soldiers from Franklin County who served in the different wars; also listed are those who died in each war.

In World War II, fourteen Franklin County men lost their lives: eleven in the army, two in the navy, and one in the marines. A representative of the local Red Cross would inform local soldiers stationed elsewhere of family news in Franklin County, and the federal government would send a telegram to the families of slain soldiers informing them of the loss of their family member.

The armory was used during World War II for the local Little United Servicemen's Organization (USO), which catered to the many soldiers temporarily assigned to train in the area. The Red Cross and the local Rationing Board also used the armory during the war. Local women spent a lot of time there wrapping bandages for use by troops overseas and also socializing with the soldiers, although strict rules governed the actions of the soldiers and women. Even so, several local women married servicemen stationed in Apalachicola.

As part of the preparations for a possible enemy invasion during World War II, the Franklin County Defense Council notified residents that, if enemy planes approached, the siren on top of the armory would sound a long blast. If an air attack occurred at night, the power company would turn off its main switch, effectively cutting all electric power in the city. A spotters' tower on top of the armory allowed local civilian women to watch for enemy airplanes, which fortunately did not show up over Franklin County.

The airfield located two miles west of town also played a

part in World War II. The facility dates back to 1934, when the Federal Emergency Relief Administration (FERA) built it during the Depression, when much of America reeled under terrible economic conditions. During World War II, as the Apalachicola Army Air Field, it served as one of two hundred such military installations in Florida and operated as a training center for aerial artillery gunners. It was the only airfield in Florida where B-29s could land. To make the field seem even more important to any German spies who might observe it, the military built wooden replicas of large planes and placed them near the airstrip. One of the men trained there was actor Clark Gable, who was assigned to Tyndall. Toward the end of the war, Maxwell Air Force Field in Montgomery, Alabama, used the base as an auxiliary field. It eventually became part of Tyndall Air Field in Panama City and changed its official name to the Army Air Forces Flexible Gunnery School.

The Franklin Guards were reorganized at a meeting in 1948. Among those attending that meeting was Roland Schoelles, who would become Sergeant First Class and serve with the unit for almost forty years.

The U-2 pilot who photographed Russian missiles on Cuban soil in the early 1960s was a local man, Richard Steve Heyser, who eventually retired in 1974 after thirty years with the U.S. Air Force. Just before he retired, he was director of World Wide Air Force U-2 Operations for the Strategic Air Command (SAC).

Among the former soldiers buried in Franklin County, several need to be mentioned. Evergreen Cemetery in Carrabelle is the final resting place of four members of one family, all of whom served in the armed forces. A father (William Squires, World War I), two of his sons (Charles Squires and Laurice Squires, World War II and Korea), and a daughter-in-law (Elizabeth Squires, World War II). A veterans' organization places a small American flag near the four gravesites, testifying to the valor of the Squires family.

James S. "Gentleman Jim" Daly may be the only person to have served in all four branches of the armed forces, plus the National Guard and the Merchant Marine. After he retired, he served for eight years as mayor and municipal judge in Apalachicola. Herbert Smith, who, after being listed twenty-two years as Missing in Action (MIA) in the Vietnam War, was buried in Magnolia Cemetery in 1988. Robert Howell was honored in the 1980s for being promoted to Brigadier General in the Florida Army National Guard—the first time that a Franklin County native reached flag rank in any branch of the service. Howell began serving as Clerk of the Circuit Court of Franklin County in 1957 and became one of the most knowledgeable persons about the county.

Another Apalachicola man honored by the military was Commander Roderick D. McLeod, who received one of the highest awards in the U.S. Navy for individual peacetime achievement in Norfolk, Virginia, the Navy Commendation Medal, for his performance as Reserve Intelligence Program Officer in Norfolk.

In 1975, the local weather service moved from the Apalachicola post office to the airport as part of a project that inaugurated three hundred weather stations across the country under the auspices of the National Oceanic and Atmospheric Administration. The weather station, which was connected to the main headquarters in Washington, D.C., warned the whole Florida Panhandle area of approaching storms, something of vital importance to the people and boats offshore.

In 1982, a woman joined the 710 Service Company of the Florida Army National Guard for the first time. Pamela Lewis, an African American from Apalachicola, broke the gender barrier and led the way for other women to join the unit.

Apalachicola may become the site of a replica of the Three Servicemen Statue, the original of which is part of the Vietnam Veterans Memorial in Washington, D.C. (For more details see chapter 22.)

The county may once again become a major training ground if a proposal is approved by the Armed Services to use the Apalachicola River area for riverine warfare training, especially by seamen like the Navy Seals in Naval Special Warfare.

CONCLUSION

A REPORT IN 2002 FROM THE University of Florida's Bureau of Economic and Business Research predicted that Florida will replace New York as the third largest state by 2024, reaching a size of about 24.5 million. Franklin County is predicted to be the smallest county in the state at that time, adding fewer than 3,000 residents.

Because Franklin County's towns along Apalachicola Bay are away from the busy I-10 highway, which runs east-west across Florida's Panhandle, the area has been relatively free of the hordes of visitors who frequent other coasts in the state.

The county's one blinking traffic light is a good symbol of The Forgotten Coast, as it tells us to slow down and relax, not stopping completely, but meandering through the town and our lives to appreciate the past, the glories of nature, the history all around us.

In a 2002 report, the Nature Conservancy estimated that development is putting tremendous pressure on Florida, that 165,000 acres of Florida land are being developed each year, a figure that works out to 452 acres a day. With so much of Franklin County still undeveloped, one can hope that planners use the land well. Because more than half of the state's seventeen million residents live in the coastal zone, Franklin County—with its relatively untapped coastline—will be under great pressure to open up to development. One can be very grateful that the state- and federal-owned lands will not be developed, but will remain in their pristine condition for all to enjoy for generations to come.

Apalachicola Bay is one of Florida's treasures from the standpoint of seafood eaters, history buffs, sunbathers, and appreciators of the simple life of bygone days. As more and more people discover the delights of this area, with its small towns and rich bay, the coast will no longer have the epithet "forgotten." Nonetheless, because of the foresight of environmentalists and governmental agencies that bought most of the county's land for preservation, it should remain relatively undeveloped.

VISITING INFORMATION

GENERAL

Apalachicola Bay Chamber of Commerce
Chamber Office and Visitor Center
122 Commerce Street
Apalachicola, FL 32320
Phone: 850-653-9419
www.apalachicolabay.org

Carrabelle Chamber of Commerce
PO Drawer DD
Carrabelle, FL 32322
Phone: 850-697-2585
www.carrabelle.org

Franklin County Government Services
http://www.franklincountyflorida.com

For information about fishing and
hunting in Franklin County, contact
Florida Fish and Wildlife Conservation Commission
Northwest Region
3911 Hwy. 2321
Panama City, FL 32409-1658
Phone: 850-265-3676
http://myfwc.com

ST. VINCENT ISLAND

For information and a brochure on the
general hunting regulations, camping
facilities, and tours, contact the Refuge
Manager at
St. Vincent National Wildlife Refuge
PO Box 447
Apalachicola, FL 32329
or contact the St. Vincent National
Wildlife Refuge Visitor Center at
Harbor Master Building
479 Market Street
Apalachicola, FL
Phone: 850-653-8808

http://southeast.fws.gov/StVincent/

For **ferry service,** contact the
Apalachicola Bay Chamber of
Commerce or
St. Vincent Island Shuttle Service at
850-229-1065,
www.stvincentisland.com.

ST. GEORGE ISLAND

Cape St. George Lighthouse
Cape St. George Island
Apalachicola, FL 32328
No telephone number available
http://users.erols.com/lthouse/csglt.htm

Dr. Julian G. Bruce St. George Island State Park
1900 E. Gulf Beach Dr.
St. George Island, Florida 32328
Phone: 850-927-2111
www.floridastateparks.org/stgeorgeisland/default.asp

St. George Inn
135 Franklin Boulevard
St. George Island, FL 32328
Phone: 850-927-2903

DOG ISLAND

Pelican Inn
PO Box 123
Apalachicola, FL 32329
Phone: 800-451-5294
www.thepelicaninn.com

APALACHICOLA RIVER

Apalachicola Bay & River Keeper, Inc. (ABARK)
29 Island Road., Suite 6
PO Box 484
Eastpoint, FL 32328

No telephone number available
www.apalachicola.com/riverkeeper/

APALACHICOLA NATIONAL ESTUARINE RESEARCH RESERVE

ANERR Nature Center
261 Seventh Street
Apalachicola, FL 32320
Phone: 850-653-8063
http://nerrs.noaa.gov/Apalachicola/

Florida Marine Research Institute
100 Eighth Avenue SE
St. Petersburg, FL 33701-5095
Phone: 727-896-8626
www.floridamarine.org.

Private boat companies take visitors on **estuary tours.** Try Apalachicola Tours at 850-653-2593.

OYSTERS

Annual Seafood Festival
Apalachicola, FL
Phone: 850-653-9419
http://www.apalachicolabay.org/

FORT GADSDEN

Fort Gadsden
Highway 65, 12 miles north off
Highway 98
Eastpoint, FL 32328
Phone: 850-670-8616
No website available.

LANARK AND ST. JAMES ISLAND

Camp Gordon Johnston Museum
302 Marine St.
Carrabelle, FL 32322
Phone: 850-697-8575
www.campgordonjohnston.com

Apalachee Ecological Conservancy, Inc.
3295 Crawfordville Highway,
Suite 6
Crawfordville, FL 32327
Phone: 850-926-5729
www.apeco.org

CARRABELLE BEACH

Tate's Hell State Forest
Florida Division of Forestry
290 Airport Road
Carrabelle, FL 32322
Phone: 850-697-3734
www.fldof.com/state_forests/Tates_Hell.htm

DOWNTOWN APALACHICOLA

Apalachicola Seafood Grill & Steakhouse
100 Market Street
Apalachicola, FL 32320
Phone: 850-653-9510
No website available

Chapman Botanical Gardens
Corner of Market Street and Martin Luther King Jr. Avenue
Apalachicola, FL 32320
No telephone number or website available

Dixie Theatre
21 Avenue E
Apalachicola, FL 32320
850-653-3200
www.dixietheatre.com.

JE Grady Building
76 Water Street
Apalachicola, FL 32320
Phone: 850-653-4099
http://www.jegrady.com/

Orman House
177 Fifth Street
Apalachicola, FL 32320
Phone: 850-653-1209
http://www.floridastateparks.org/orma
nhouse/default.asp

Raney House
Avenue F at Market Street
Apalachicola, FL 32320
No telephone number or
website available

INNS AND HOTELS

Adolph Flatauer House
Gulf State Community Bank
73 Avenue E
Apalachicola, FL 32320
Phone: 850-653-2126
http://www.gscb.com

Coombs House Inn
80 Sixth Street
Apalachicola, FL 32320
Phone: 850-653-9199
www.coombshouseinn.com

The Gibson Inn
PO Box 221
Apalachicola, FL 32329
Phone: 850-653-2191
www.gibsoninn.com

Henry Brash House
67 Avenue D
Apalachicola, FL 32320
No telephone number or
website available

Marks/Clark House
65 Avenue E
Apalachicola, FL 32320
No telephone number or
website available

CHURCHES

Trinity Church/Historic Tour of Homes
79 Sixth Street
Apalachicola, FL 32320
Phone: 850-653-9550
http://www.diocgc.org/cong/2.htm

PARKS

Battery Park
Avenue B between Fifth and Sixth
Streets
Apalachicola, FL 32320
No telephone number or
website available

Lafayette Park
Avenue B between 13th and 15th
Streets
Apalachicola, FL 32320
No telephone number or
website available

Villa Rosa (Alexander Key's Home)
15 13th Street
Apalachicola, FL 32320
No telephone number or
website available

JOHN GORRIE MUSEUM AND CHAPMAN HOUSE

The John Gorrie Museum
46 Sixth St.
Apalachicola, FL 32320
Phone: 850-653-9347
www.floridastateparks.org/johngor-
riemuseum/default.asp

FURTHER READING

Scott Andree, ed. *Apalachicola Oyster Industry.* Gainesville, Florida: Florida Sea Grant College, 1983.

Apalachicola Bay: Aquatic Preserve Management Plan. Tallahassee, Florida: Department of Natural Resources, 1992.

Joseph Bechton. "Old Hickory and the Negro Fort," *Pensacola History Illustrated,* vol. 2, no. 2 (fall 1986): pp. 25–32.

Raymond B. Becker. *John Gorrie, M.D.* New York, New York: Carlton, 1972.

Kevin Begos. "Round Trip Ticket: Apalachicola to New York, and back," *The News Herald,* (November 12, 1998): pp. 3GF.

Peggy Bennett. *The Varmints.* New York, New York: Knopf, 1946. This is a novel about the Apalachicola area by a local author.

Morris Bishop. *The Odyssey of Cabeza de Vaca.* New York: Century Company, New York, 1933. This is a book about the Narváez expedition.

Mark F. Boyd. "Events at Prospect Bluff on the Apalachicola River, 1808–1818," *Florida Historical Quarterly,* vol. 16 (October 1937): pp. 55–96.

Kenneth Brower. "Can of Worms," *The Atlantic Monthly,* vol. 283, no. 3 (March 1999): pp. 91–100. This is an article about worm grunting.

Henry Cabbage. "The Apalachicola River: 108 Miles of Fun," *Florida Wildlife,* vol. 55, no. 3 (May-June, 2001): pp. 2–5. This is a book about hunting, fishing, and camping along the river.

David J. Coles. "'Hell-by-the-Sea': Florida's Camp Gordon Johnston in World War II," *Florida Historical Quarterly.* vol. 73, no. 1 (July, 1994): pp. 1–22.

Joe and Monica Cook. *River Song: A Journey down the Chattahoochee and Apalachicola Rivers.* Tuscaloosa, Alabama: University of Alabama Press, 2000.

James W. Covington. "The Negro Fort," *Gulf Coast Historical Review,* vol. 5, no. 2 (spring 1990): pp. 78–91.

Joseph D. Cushman, Jr. "The Blockade and Fall of Apalachicola, 1861–1862," *Florida Historical Quarterly,* vol. 41, no. 1 (July 1962): pp. 38–46.

T. Frederick Davis. "Pioneer Florida," *Florida Historical Quarterly,* vol. 23, no. 1 (July 1944): pp. 177–183. This is an article about the first railroads.

Jane Doerfer. "Starting at the top," *House Beautiful,* vol. 137, no. 9 (September 1995): pp. 94–99. This is an article about a former cypress mill in Apalachicola that became a beautiful home.

Audrey Dunham. "Tales of Tate's Hell," *Geojourney,* vol. 1, no. 2 (October, 1980): pp. 8–9.

Robin F.A. Fabel, ed. and trans. *Shipwreck and Adventures of Monsieur Pierre Viaud.* Pensacola, Florida: University of West Florida, 1990.

Connie May Fowler. *Remembering Blue*. New York, New York: Doubleday, 2000. This is a novel set partially on the fictional island of Lethe, which represents Dog Island.

Jennifer Greer. "Handle With Care," *Southern Living,* vol. 30 (August 1995), p. 36. This is an article about the red-cockaded woodpecker in the Apalachicola Forest.

Gerald Grow. "Florida in 2001: The Environment," *Geojourney,* vol. 2, no. 3 (summer, 1982): p. 14–15.

Rubylea Hall. *God Has a Sense of Humor*. New York, New York: Duell, Sloan, 1960. This is a novel about the Apalachicola River country.

William F. Heavey. *Down Ramp! The Story of the Army Amphibian Engineers.* Nashville: The Battery Press, 1988.

Carol M. Highsmith and Ted Landphair. *America Restored*. Washington, DC: The Preservation Press, 1994–.

William Temple Hornaday. *A Mon-o-graph on St. Vincent's Game Preserve.* Buffalo, New York: 1909. This is a book about Dr. Ray Pierce's development of the island.

Bruce Hunt. *Visiting Small-Town Florida,* Revised Edition, Sarasota, Florida: Pineapple Press, 2003.

Gloria Jahoda. *The Other Florida*. New York, New York: Charles Scribner's Sons, 1967.

G.F. Jordan. "Reef Formation in the Gulf of Mexico off Apalachicola Bay, Florida," *Bulletin of the Geological Society of America,* vol. 63 (July, 1952): pp. 741–744.

Wallace Kaufman and Orrin H. Pilkey, Jr. *The Beaches Are Moving: The Drowning of America's Shoreline,* Durham, North Carolina: Duke University Press, 1983.

Alexander Key, *Island Light*. Indianapolis, Indiana: Bobbs-Merrill, 1950. This is a novel about Little St. George Island and the lighthouse.

——.*The Wrath and the Wind*. Indianapolis, Indiana: Bobbs-Merrill, 1949. This is a novel about slave trading in Apalachicola.

Stanley Kirkland. "Experience the Apalachicola River WEA," *Florida Wildlife,* vol. 54, no. 1 (January–February, 2000): pp. 28–30.

——. "The Apalachicola River: Winding Through History," *Florida Wildlife,* vol. 55, no. 3 (May-June, 2001): pp. 6–7.

——. "The Steamboat Era on the Apalachicola, Chattahoochee and Flint rivers," *Florida Wildlife,* vol. 55, no. 3 (May-June, 2001): pp. 9–11.

Jeff Klinkenberg. *Real Florida*. Asheboro, North Carolina: Down Home Press, 1993.

Robert J. Livingston. *Dog Island: A Barrier Island Ecosystem*. Tallahassee, Florida: Florida State University, 1991.

———. *Resource Atlas of the Apalachicola Estuary.* Gainesville, Florida: Florida Sea Grant College, 1983.

Del and Marty Marth, eds. *The Rivers of Florida.* Sarasota, Florida: Pineapple Press, 1990.

Cora Mitchel. *Reminiscences of the Civil War.* Providence, Rhode Island: Snow & Farnham Company, 1916. This book is about life in Apalachicola through the 1860s and is written by the daughter of a cotton merchant.

Edward Mueller. *Perilous Journeys: A History of Steamboating on the Chattahoochee, Apalachicola and Flint Rivers, 1828–1928.* Eufaula, Alabama: Historic Chattahoochee Commission, 1990.

Jimmie Nichols. "Dr. Chapman, Botanist, Was 19th Century Apalach Hero," *The News Herald,* November 26, 1998: pp. 4GF.

———. "A Look Back at Public Schools in Franklin," *The News Herald,* Dec. 3, 1998: pp. 5GF.

———. *1836–1986. Sesquicentennial History of Trinity Episcopal Church, Apalachicola, Florida.* Apalachicola, Florida: Trinity Church, 1987.

Jimmie J. Nichols. "Apalachicola man keeping local history alive," *The News Herald,* June 25, 1998: p. 3GF.

Barbara A. Noe, ed. *Guide to Small Town Escapes.* Washington, District of Columbia: National Geographic Society, 2000.

Parke Puterbaugh and Alan Bisbort. *Florida Beaches.* Santa Rosa, California: Foghorn Press, 1999.

Anthony F. Randazzo and Douglas S. Jones, eds. *The Geology of Florida.* Gainesville, Florida: University Presses of Florida, 1997.

William Warren Rogers. *Outposts on the Gulf: Saint George Island and Apalachicola from Early Exploration to World War II.* Pensacola, Florida: University of West Florida, 1986.

William Warren Rogers and Lee Willis, III. *At the Water's Edge: A Pictorial and Narrative History of Apalachicola and Franklin County.* Virginia Beach, Virginia: Donning Company, 1997.

C.J. Schade. *Late Holocene Sedimentology of St. George Island, Florida.* Tallahassee, Florida: Florida State University, 1985. (M.S. thesis, Department of Geology).

Steven G. Seibert. "Apalachicola Black Bears," *Florida Wildlife,* vol. 51, no. 4 (July-August, 1997): pp. 16–19.

V.M. (Vivian) Sherlock. *The Fever Man.* Tallahassee, Florida: Medallion Press, 1982.

Vivian M. Sherlock, "Medical Practices in the Port of Apalachicola, 1830–1850," *Apalachee* (publication of the Tallahassee Historical Society), vol. 9 (1984): pp. 97–104.

Celestine Sibley. *Straight as an Arrow.* New York, New York: HarperCollins, 1992.

Frank Slaughter. *Storm Haven.* Garden City, New York: Doubleday, 1953. This is a novel about the Apalachicola River area during the Civil War.

"St. Vincent Island," *Florida Wildlife,* vol. 23, no. 4 (September, 1969): pp. 10–15; vol. 23, no. 5 (October, 1969): pp. 12–17.

Don Stap. "Florida's Ancient Shores," *Audubon,* vol. 97, no. 3 (May-June, 1995): pp. 36–37.

Steamboats in 19th Century Florida, Florida Heritage Education Program, Series 2, Number 19, November, 1997.

Frank Stephenson and Bruce Ritchie. "Second Chance," *Florida State University Research in Review* (winter 2003): pp. 26–37.

Mike Stewart. *Dog Island.* New York, New York: G.P. Putnam's Sons, 2000.

H. Marshall Taylor. "John Gorrie: Physician, Scientist, Inventor," *The Southern Medical Journal,* vol. 28, no. 12 (December, 1935): pp. 1075–1082.

Dr. Kris W. Thoemke. "Can Our Estuaries Survive the 80s?" *Geojourney,* vol. 1, no. 3 (December, 1980): pp. 4–7.

Maxine Turner. *Navy Gray: A Story of the Confederate Navy on the Chattahoochee and Apalachicola Rivers.* Tuscaloosa, Alabama: University of Alabama Press, 1988.

George Norton Wakefield. *A Florida Sandpiper, Or A Fool Rushed In Where Angels Fear to Tread.* Gainesville, Florida: Storter Printing Company, 1982. This is an autobiography of an agriculture teacher who grew up and attended the Episcopal Church in Apalachicola.

Nancy White, Terry Simpson, Suella McMillan. *Apalachicola Valley Archaeology.* Apalachicola, Florida: W.T. Neal Civic Center and Apalachicola National Estuarine Research Reserve, 1998.

Robert Wilder. *Bright Feather.* New York, New York: Putnam, 1948. This is a book about the Seminole Indian Wars in the area.

Marlene Womack. *War Comes to Florida's Northern Gulf Coast.* Panama City, Florida: Womack Publications, 2002.

Dorothy Worley. *Enchanted Harbor.* New York, New York: Avalon, 1956. This is a novel about a counterfeiting ring in Apalachicola.

Jessica Zimmer. "Howling at a Florida Moon," *EcoFlorida,* vol. 2, no. 4 (winter, 2001): pp. 7–9. This is an article on the extinction of red wolves on St. Vincent Island.

INDEX